GREAT THINGS

GW01551286

COOKIN'
IN
VENTURA

BY

GAIL HOBBS

GOLD COAST PRESS

Great Things Are
COOKIN' IN VENTURA.

ISBN 0-9642012-0-8

Published June 1994.
Manufactured in the United States of America.

GOLD COAST PRESS
4360 E. MAIN ST., SUITE 129,
VENTURA, CA. 93003

ACKNOWLEDGMENTS

Many people assisted in the creation of this book. All of your contributions are greatly appreciated.

The following people deserve special recognition:

Thank you to all the creative chefs and restaurant owners for your time and for sharing some of your most valued recipes.

Special thanks to Pete Veltre of the Black & White Lab of Ventura for expert photo guidance. I couldn't have done it without you.

Thanks to Andrew Caffrey and Mavis Caffrey for editing advice, to Betty Dorian who unknowingly inspired this book and the late Russ Smith of the Ventura Visitors Bureau for his encouragement.

Most of all, thanks to my husband, Don for his unending support in so many ways.

* * * * * * *

DEDICATION

This book is dedicated to all those who have ever needed a helping hand.

America is in turmoil. We must reach out to help one another if we are to survive.

We can no longer count on the government to solve all of our social problems.

Community problem solving must begin at the individual and business level.

Gold Coast Press will donate five percent of the company's gross sales of this book to a local charity.

* * * * * * *

RECIPE GUIDE

SWEET ENDINGS:

* * * * * * *

RESTAURANT GUIDE

* * * * * * *

POINTS OF INTEREST

PHOTOGRAPHS

* * * * * *

The San Buenaventura City Hall and bronze statue of
Father Serra.

* * * * * * *

WELCOME TO VENTURA!

Historic Ventura is on California's Gold Coast in between Los Angeles and Santa Barbara. In this beautiful beach town, locals and visitors always find fun things to do and interesting places to see.

Thanks to a year-round mild climate, outdoor activities are plentiful. Golf, tennis, walking, biking, surfing, sailing, fishing and camping are enjoyed by many. Twenty five miles of bike paths and walkways, almost two dozen parks and of course, the sand and surf, are all open for public use.

Art and culture are abundant in San Buenaventura, one of California's oldest established cities. From the Albinger Archaeological Museum to the fully restored San Buenaventura City Hall and the Olivas Adobe, it is apparent that the past is not forgotten. Superb art galleries and the walls of local restaurants are where Ventura artists display their talents. Live concerts and plays attract music and theater fans. Ventura is a festival lover's paradise. There are several each month including the California Beach Party and the Holiday Street Festival.

Downtown's antique and second hand shops, the Harbor Village boutiques and the newly renovated Buenaventura Mall are a shopper's dream come true.

The city is home to over 200 eateries, from fine gourmet dining to casual bistros, it's all here. Fresh fish, steaks, tacos, burgers, pizza, cheesecake and cappuccino, along with many ethnic dishes, aim to please the most discriminating palates.

For a relaxing holiday, a fun filled adventure or a lifetime of pleasure, locals and visitors all agree, Ventura can't be beat!

* * * * * *

THE NEW
PIERPONT INN
BY THE SEA

The PIERPONT INN, a designated historical landmark, has been well known for spectacular views of it's beautiful flower gardens, the Pacific Ocean, the Channel Islands and the Ventura Pier.

The Inn was built by the Pierpont family of Ojai in 1908 and had several owners until purchased by the Gleichmann family in 1928. They spent 10 years renovating the neglected 24 room complex and have since always maintained a dignified hotel and restaurant.

The PIERPONT INN has an impressive guest list including many celebrities such as Jane Fonda, James Garner, Roy Rogers, Dale Evans and George and Barbara Bush, who first visited in 1949.

Louis Ludwig, the Inn's Executive Chef, is the third to be employed by the family owned and managed restaurant since 1928. His Cioppino recipe has just recently won 3rd Overall, 3rd in People's Choice and 1st Place in Presentation at the Cio-Pinot Cook-off held annually at the Old Port Inn in Avila Beach.

One way to sample the best food that Ludwig and the PIERPONT have to offer is to attend one of their Winemaker Dinners. Traditionally these feasts were to celebrate the last crushed grape of the wine harvest where winemakers, hunters and merchants served their finest wines and foods. Today, whether attending a special Winemaker Dinner or enjoying a meal in the restaurant, guests are treated to superb food and attentive service.

* * * * * * *

Pierpont Beach Clam Chowder

6 STRIPS BACON, CHOPPED FINE
2 CUPS YELLOW ONIONS, 1/4 INCH DICE
2 CUPS CELERY, 1/4 INCH DICE
1 TBSP. FRESH GARLIC, MINCED
2 TSP. DRIED THYME LEAVES
1/4 LB. WHOLE BUTTER
1 CUP ALL-PURPOSE FLOUR
1 PINT HEAVY CREAM
2 TSP. FRESH GROUND BLACK PEPPER
6 CANS CHOPPED CLAMS (OR 6 DOZEN
    FRESH LITTLE NECKS)
3 CUPS POTATOES, PEELED, 1 INCH DICE
    AND BLANCHED
2 TSP. CELERY SALT
2 TBSP. FRESH PARSLEY, CHOPPED FINE

Brown bacon in a heavy stock pot (6 to 8 quarts). Add onions, celery, garlic, thyme and butter. Sauté until celery is tender.

Stir in flour and simmer on medium low heat for 20 minutes stirring regularly to avoid scorching.

Preheat cream to just under a boil. Stir hot cream into sautéed mixture and add black pepper and just the strained juice of the canned clams.

Add diced blanched potatoes, celery salt and parsley. Simmer on medium low heat for one hour or until potatoes have softened. Stir in strained chopped clams and simmer for 20 minutes. Makes one gallon.

* * * * * * *

Louis Ludwig, Executive Chef for the PIERPONT INN and Brett Jonas, one of his two chefs, developed this clam chowder recipe, which is said to be the best in Southern California.

Hazelnut Chicken

4 BONELESS, SKINLESS CHICKEN BREASTS
1 CUP EGG WASH (3 EGGS MIXED WITH
  2/3 CUP MILK)
1 CUP SEASONED FLOUR (FLOUR, SALT
  AND PEPPER)
1 CUP BREAD CRUMBS
1 CUP HAZELNUTS, ROASTED AND
  CHOPPED FINE
1/4 CUP OLIVE OIL
1 1/2 TO 2 CUPS HOT SHERRIED
  HAZELNUT SAUCE

Dip chicken breasts in egg wash and then in seasoned flour. Allow coating to form and set for 15 minutes.

Dip coated chicken breasts again in egg wash. Combine bread crumbs and hazelnuts. Bread coated chicken by pressing breading mixture firmly so that both sides of chicken are coated evenly.

Heat olive oil in a sauté pan over medium heat and sauté chicken to a golden brown on each side, taking care to cook each breast all the way through.

Top Hazelnut Chicken with hot Sherried Hazelnut Sauce.

Makes four generous servings.

* * * * * * *

Serve Hazelnut Chicken with mashed potatoes or rice also topped with hot Sherried Hazelnut Sauce. Accompany with fresh vegetables.

Sherried Hazelnut Sauce

1 CUP WHITE SAUCE
3 TBSP. MINCED SHALLOTS
1/4 CUP HAZELNUT OIL
1/2 CUP SHERRY
3 TBSP. DIJON MUSTARD
1/2 CUP HAZELNUTS, ROASTED AND
    CHOPPED FINE

Heat white sauce to a soft simmer.

In a separate pan sauté shallots in hazelnut oil until tender. Add sherry, Dijon mustard and hazelnuts. Simmer at a soft boil for 15 minutes.

Stir sautéed mixture into the white sauce and continue to simmer for another 10 to 15 minutes.

Makes 2 cups of sauce for Hazelnut Chicken.

* * * * * * *

Louis Ludwig, Executive Chef at the PIERPONT INN suggests a chilled glass of Sauvignon Blanc to complement Hazelnut Chicken.

The food at the PIERPONT INN has always been considered outstanding in quality and consistent with the times. They are probably best known for this Hazelnut Chicken with the sherried Dijon cream sauce, Rack of Lamb and fresh seafood.

Rice Perloo with Peach Chutney

1 CUP CONVERTED RICE
2 TBSP. BUTTER
1/2 TSP. SALT
1/8 TSP. SAFFRON
3/4 CUP GREEN PEPPER, DICED
1/2 CUP ONION, MINCED
3 CUPS CHICKEN STOCK
1 CUP HAM, DICED
1 CUP COOKED CHICKEN MEAT, DICED
1 CUP COOKED, PEELED SHRIMP, CLEANED
1/2 CUP CORN KERNELS, FRESH OR
  FROZEN
1/2 CUP EARLY PEAS, FRESH OR FROZEN

Using a heavy sauce pot with a lid, sauté rice in butter until slightly browned. Add salt, saffron, green pepper and onion. Continue to sauté until pepper and onion are tender, 10 to 15 minutes, over medium high heat.

Add chicken stock and bring to a boil. Cover and reduce to a very low simmer for 10 to 15 minutes, or until rice is nearly done and has absorbed most of the liquid.

Gently fold in diced ham and chicken, shrimp, corn and peas. Cover and allow to steam for another 10 to 15 minutes on a very low flame.

Serve Rice Perloo immediately in a serving bowl with Peach Chutney.

* * * * * * *

A passion of the PIERPONT INN'S Chef Louis Ludwig, Southern cooking is a melting pot of international cuisine - English, German, Irish, French, Spanish and Indian.

Peach Chutney

1 LB. FRESH OR FROZEN PEACH SLICES
1 LB. SUGAR
1/2 CUP VINEGAR
1 TBSP. SALT

Combine all ingredients together in a heavy 3 quart sauce pot and heat to a simmering boil, uncovered. Avoid rapid boiling as the chutney is easily scorched.

Continue cooking until liquid is reduced by half in volume, down to about a quart, stirring occasionally. Depending on the quality of the pot and the burner used, to reach a rather thick consistency should take about 1 1/2 to 2 hours.

Store chutney in the refrigerator or in sterilized glass jars. Makes 1 quart.

* * * * * *

Chef Louis Ludwig recommends White Zinfandel, a sweet, fruity wine to accompany Rice Perloo with Peach Chutney.

Peach Chutney may be served hot or cold and is also an excellent accompaniment to meat, fish or fowl, especially which has been barbecued or blackened.

PCH One Cioppino

2 OZ. OLIVE OIL
6 CLOVES GARLIC, SLIVERED
2 TBSP. ANCHOVY PASTE
3/4 CUP WHITE ONION, 1/4 INCH DICE
3/4 CUP CELERY, 1/4 INCH DICE
2 CUPS WHITE ITALIAN WINE
4 CUPS FISH STOCK
2 - 14 1/2 OZ. CANS SLICED STEWED
   TOMATOES
1/2 LB. SQUID, BODY CLEANED, SLICED AND
   TENTACLES WHOLE
1 LB. WHITEFISH, 1 INCH CUBED FILETS
32 16/21 SHRIMP, PEELED AND DEVEINED,
   TAIL-ON
32 CLAMS, WHOLE TUA TUA OR MANILA
32 MUSSELS, PACIFIC SELECT
2 TBSP. FRESH BASIL, CHOPPED FINE
2 TBSP. FRESH OREGANO, CHOPPED FINE
2 TSP. FRESH THYME, CHOPPED FINE
2 TSP. LEMON PEPPER SEASONING

Using an 8 quart stock pot, heat olive oil on medium and sauté garlic and anchovy paste until lightly browned. Add onion and celery and sauté until translucent.

Add white wine, fish stock (canned or fresh) and sliced stewed tomatoes and simmer for 20 minutes.

Add squid, whitefish, shrimp, clams, mussels, herbs and seasonings. Cover tightly and simmer on low heat for 20 minutes.

Makes eight delicious servings.

* * * * * *

Houses on the Ventura Keys enjoy boat docks at their back doors and mountain views.

* * * * * * *

THE CHART HOUSE

STEAKS – SEAFOOD – PRIME RIB

THE CHART HOUSE restaurant, on the Ventura coast, offers a romantic view of the beautiful Pacific Ocean and the Channel Islands from every dining table. This modern dinner house was designed and built in 1981 by well known architect, Joe Lancore. THE CHART HOUSE company began in 1969 with a small eatery and bar in Aspen, Colorado and has grown to 65 restaurants throughout the United States.

Diners enjoy a wonderful meal beginning with a delicious appetizer or a trip to the almost mile long salad bar which features homemade salad dressings. The company's Paradise Bakery in San Diego supplies the fresh sourdough and a honey and molasses dark bread. Entrées include a bone-in, extra thick prime rib, hand-carved steaks such as the New York steak and filet mignon and a variety of fresh seafood. Leaving room for a sweet ending is a must. THE CHART HOUSE Mud Pie is an old favorite.

THE CHART HOUSE motto, "GREAT FOOD, GREAT SERVICE, OR IT'S ON US!" is part of what draws local Venturans and visitors to experience magnificent sunsets from this premier restaurant while dining in casual elegance.

* * * * * * *

The Chart House Blue Cheese Salad Dressing

3/4 CUP SOUR CREAM
1/2 TSP. DRY MUSTARD
1/2 TSP. BLACK PEPPER
1/2 TSP. SALT, SCANT
1/3 TSP. GARLIC POWDER, SCANT
1 TSP. WORCHESTERSHIRE SAUCE
1 1/3 CUPS MAYONNAISE
4 OZ. CRUMBLED IMPORTED DANISH BLUE
CHEESE

In a mixing bowl, combine sour cream, dry mustard, pepper, salt, garlic powder and Worchestershire sauce. Blend for 2 minutes at low speed.

Add mayonnaise and blend for 30 seconds at low speed, then increase speed to medium and blend for an additional 2 minutes.

Slowly add blue cheese and blend at low speed no longer than 4 minutes.

Refrigerate for 24 hours before serving to enhance flavor. Makes 2 1/2 cups.

* * * * * * *

The CHART HOUSE Blue Cheese Salad Dressing is a delicious alternative to ranch dressing. It may be served with a cheese and fruit platter or various deep fried appetizers such as mushrooms, zucchini, and mozzarella cheese sticks.

The Chart House Mud Pie

4 1/2 OZ. CHOCOLATE WAFERS
1/4 CUP BUTTER, MELTED
1 GALLON COFFEE ICE CREAM, SOFT
1 1/2 CUPS FUDGE SAUCE
WHIPPED CREAM
DICED ALMONDS

Crush wafers and add butter. Mix well. Press into a 9" pie plate. Pile high with soft coffee ice cream.

Top with cold fudge sauce. (It helps to put the fudge sauce in the freezer for a while to make spreading easier.)

Store the Mud Pie in the freezer for approximately 10 hours before serving.

PRESENTATION: Slice the Mud Pie into eight portions and serve on chilled dessert plates. Top with whipped cream and diced almonds.

* * * * * * *

A steaming cup of freshly brewed Kona coffee and a slice of THE CHART HOUSE Famous Mud Pie is a sinfully delicious finale to a wonderful meal.

The Peirano Building was built in 1877 and is Ventura's oldest commercial brick building. It was a grocery store until 1987.

* * * * * * *

NONA'S COURTYARD CAFÉ

BELLA MAGGIORE INN

Step back in time. Retreat to a serene hide-a-way surrounded by the vine-covered brick walls of the historic Bella Maggiore Inn. In NONA'S COURTYARD CAFÉ the sounds of the outside world are left far behind and diners are treated to a cascading water fountain and lush tropical plants.

This charming café was created in the fall of 1993 by Jonathan Enabnit. He has designed the menu to feature splendid meals embracing fresh seafood and pasta creations topped with light creamy sauces. These are the result of a fusion between California and Northern Italian cuisines. Traditional sandwiches are made from the highest quality fresh meats and vegetables and may be served on NONA'S own freshly baked Focaccia Bread.

NONA'S outdoor café is tucked away in downtown Ventura, only three blocks from the beach and the pier. It was planned to reflect the European motif and ambiance of the Bella Maggiore Inn. The original building dates back to the 1920's and was designed by architect Albert C. Martin, who also created Ventura's magnificent City Hall and Hollywood's Grauman's Chinese Theater. In 1986 the Bella Maggiore was renovated and now boasts a tastefully decorated lobby with fine antiques, a 1906 Steinway grand piano and cozy fireplace.

Escape to NONA'S COURTYARD CAFÉ, one of Ventura's best kept secrets and forget your troubles while indulging in fine food and excellent service.

* * * * * * *

Fresh Baked Focaccia Bread

3 OZ. DRY YEAST
3 CUPS WARM WATER (100°F)
16 CUPS ALL-PURPOSE FLOUR
16 TSP. OLIVE OIL
8 TSP. HONEY
1 TBSP. SALT
1 CUP FRESH GRATED PARMESAN CHEESE
2 CUPS COLD WATER

FOR TOPPING: OLIVE OIL, CRUSHED
GARLIC, FRESH CHOPPED THYME, FRESH
CHOPPED ROSEMARY

Mix yeast with warm water. Add flour, olive oil, honey, salt, parmesan cheese and cold water. Mix well.

Lightly flour table top and coat sheet pan with olive oil. Roll out dough with a rolling pin and transfer to sheet pan.

Puncture dough with fingers or fork and coat the top of dough with olive oil and crushed garlic. Lightly sprinkle with fresh thyme and fresh rosemary.

Let dough rise for approximately 2 hours.

Bake at 400 degrees for approximately 25 minutes, checking frequently. Allow to cool for 1/2 hour.

* * * * * * *

This delicious bread is ideal for sandwiches or on its own. Nona's serves their freshly baked Focaccia the traditional way, with a side of olive oil spiced with pesto and crushed red pepper.

SHIELDS BREWING CO.

"SOUTHERN CALIFORNIA'S LOCAL MICROBREWERY"

SHIELDS BREWING COMPANY, located in the heart of historic downtown Ventura, is Ventura County's first brewery since prohibition. This unique pub and grill produces eight different "hand crafted beers like days of old" behind large easy viewing windows for all to see.

Seasonal brews are available on tap in the full service restaurant and the ales that are for sale in bottles to go include Channel Islands Ale, Channel Islands Wheat, Gold Coast Beer and Shields Stout. The beers are available statewide and will soon be debuting in Coeur d'Alene, Idaho. Most impressive is the fact that SHIELDS BREWING COMPANY has just licensed the Chengdu Brewery in China to make and sell SHIELDS' Gold Coast Ale. To further put Ventura on the map, the Chinese Ale label will feature familiar Ventura sites such as the two trees and the pier.

Many items on the food menu are made with beer, including their own Whole Grain Beer Bread, Beer Batter for Fresh Veggies, Spaghetti with Ale Sauce and Southern Bread Pudding with Caramel Ale Sauce. Patrons never feel left out during the holidays as the brewery is quick to join in the festivities. They serve green beer and Corned Beef and Cabbage (made with beer, of course) on St. Paddy's Day.

The SHIELDS BREWING COMPANY has been in operation since 1990 and maintains an industrial feeling in a restaurant that is comfortable for all ages.

* * * * * * *

26

Channel Islands Beer Batter

1 TBSP. BAKING POWDER
1/4 TBSP. BAKING SODA
1 TBSP. SEASONING SALT
1/4 TBSP. ONION POWDER
1/4 TBSP. WHITE PEPPER
1/2 TBSP. GARLIC POWDER
1/3 CUP CORNSTARCH
2 EGGS
1 22 OZ. BOTTLE CHANNEL ISLANDS ALE
WHITE FLOUR

LARGE BROWN ONIONS, SLICED
ASSORTED FRESH VEGETABLES: CARROTS,
    BROCCOLI, CAULIFLOWER, MUSHROOMS,
    ETC. ALL CLEANED AND CUT INTO LARGE
    BITE SIZED PIECES.

Separate egg whites and set aside.

Beat egg yolks and remaining ingredients (except flour) together. Add flour until the consistency of pancake-type batter is reached. Chill for 1 hour in the refrigerator.

Just before use, whip egg whites until stiff and fold into batter.

Heat oil in a deep fryer to 165° to 170°.

Hand dip onion rings or vegetables into beer batter, separate and drop into hot oil one by one. Deep fry until golden brown.

Serve with ranch dressing or ketchup, if desired.

* * * * * * *

The Old Town Livery was built in 1906. It now houses
an arts center, a coffee bar and antique shops.

* * * * * * *

HISTORIC DOWNTOWN VENTURA

The heart and soul of San Buenaventura lies in the downtown community. This bustling section of Ventura is full of life as locals and visitors walk the streets, exploring every nook and cranny, searching for hidden treasures.

Shopaholics will delight in wandering through some 25 antique shops, numerous second-hand boutiques, book stores, and many more specialty shops such as Atelier de Chocolat, a European Chocolate Boutique. Each is filled to the brim with collectables, jewelry, hand-made wares, clothes and even a few modern artifacts.

Tucked between the shops are coffee bars like Café Voltaire in the old Livery courtyard, and charming restaurants such as Franky's, 66 California and Nona's Courtyard Café in the historic Bella Maggiore Inn. Each fascinating eatery has a unique ambiance, a story of it's own and a delicious meal to satisfy the most demanding of critics.

History buffs will be drawn to tour diversely cultural Main Street. The San Buenaventura Mission (founded by Father Serra in 1782), the Archaeological Museum, the Ventura County Museum of History and Art and the Ortega Adobe Historic Residence (built in 1857 and where The Ortega Chili Co. began in the 1890's), are filled with interesting exhibits.

The downtown is the site of local parades, street fairs where artists sell their hand-crafted wares and the popular Saturday morning Farmer's Market. Whether out to shop for something special, have a bite to eat, or just cruise the area - historic downtown Ventura will always delight visitors.

* * * * * * *

CAFÉ
VOLTAIRE

CAFÉ VOLTAIRE is a real European-style coffee house in the courtyard of the Livery Arts Center, one of Ventura's oldest buildings. The downtown coffee bar brews freshly ground, locally roasted gourmet coffees. A traditional cup is always available as well as the more contemporary flavors and concoctions.

Customers may sit at one of the small indoor tables or in the fresh air courtyard. Their new Global Lunch is prepared by Tony Palk, a retired British film editor and former owner and head chef of The Birtley Hotel in Bournmouth, England. Chef Tony offers a different international special daily including Sheperd's Pie, traditional English pub grub and the French Chicken á la King, along with soups, salads and sandwiches.

In the corner of this artsy café stands a large bookcase crammed with old books for anyone to browse through. Local artists hang their works on the walls and display handcrafted sculptures around the room, hoping to invite a sale.

Evenings at CAFÉ VOLTAIRE are filled with poetry readings, live music and friendly chess games. Several nights a week customers are encouraged to join in and grab the microphone to try their hand at entertaining.

A stroll around historic downtown Ventura wouldn't be complete without stopping at CAFÉ VOLTAIRE for a cup of steaming java or a home cooked lunch.

* * * * * * *

Chicken á la King

2 OZ. BUTTER
1 SMALL ONION, PEELED AND FINELY
  CHOPPED
8 OZ. MUSHROOMS, WASHED AND HALVED
2 TBSP. CORNFLOWER
1/2 PINT HALF AND HALF
1/2 PINT CHICKEN STOCK
1 LB. COOKED CHICKEN, DICED
PINCH DRIED THYME
1 TBSP. DRY SHERRY
SALT AND WHITE PEPPER TO TASTE

Melt butter in a sauté pan, add onion and gently sauté until tender. Add the mushrooms and sauté for 3 minutes.

Sprinkle in the cornflower and continue cooking for one minute more. Stir in half and half and chicken stock. Bring to a boil, stirring constantly.

Add chicken, thyme, sherry and season to taste with salt and pepper. Simmer for 35 minutes.

Serves 6 to 8.

* * * * * * *

Delicious served over a bed of rice or with mashed potatoes.

FRANKY'S

FRANKY'S RESTAURANT in downtown Ventura, boasts "We Serve Only The Finest, Freshest, Healthiest Food!" One glance at the menu proves it. Although not a vegetarian restaurant, don't look for the beef here, there isn't any!

What you will find is a large selection of delicious, healthy meals such as the Sante Fe Omelet or pancakes for breakfast. Lunch choices are turkey burgers, homemade soups, sandwiches and pitas (like the Buenaventura with buena beans, crunchies, tomato, chives, Cheddar cheese and mayo). FRANKY'S uses only natural seasonings, NO MSG.

Kris Pustina, FRANKY'S owner for the past 6 years, enhances customer satisfaction by serving homemade desserts and muffins using the healthiest ingredients available. A hot cappuccino, cold beer or glass of fine wine is a refreshing way to complement each meal.

Greeting guests at the front door of FRANKY'S are the models for their unusual logo. Two tall, bronze frog statues, that appear to have been frozen in time, are the work of local sculptor, Paul Lindard. They pose on a slab of Italian marble and walnut, fashioned by Kris' husband. The restaurant is decorated with the works of local artists. Handmade quilts warm a long brick wall lined with booths. Paintings and pottery are also displayed for 6 to 8 weeks at a time before the exhibit changes. All are available for purchase.

Dining alone or with a friend, FRANKY'S friendly staff makes every patron comfortable.

* * * * * * *

Curried Chicken Salad

1 LB. DICED CHICKEN, LIGHT AND DARK
   MEAT
1 HEAPING TSP. CURRY POWDER
1/2 TSP. GARLIC POWDER
1/2 TSP. COARSE GROUND BLACK PEPPER
1 TSP. CHICKEN BASE (NO MSG)
1 GRANNY SMITH APPLE, DICED
MAYONNAISE TO TASTE

Mix all ingredients together.

Stir in mayonnaise according to personal taste.

* * * * * * *

Franky's Curried Chicken Salad is delicious in a pita or nestled in a bed of crisp greens. It is a refreshing alternative to tuna salad.

Franky's Turkey Burgers

2 LBS. GROUND TURKEY
2 TSP. BASIL
1 TSP. ITALIAN SEASONING
2 EGGS
1/2 TSP. LIQUID SMOKE
1 TSP. GARLIC POWDER
1 TBSP. CHICKEN BASE (NO MSG)

Combine all ingredients and mix well.

Form into patties and cook through.

Serve on whole grain buns and add your favorite toppings.

Superb grilled on the BBQ!

Prepare to enjoy the best Turkey Burger you'll ever eat!

* * * * * * *

FRANKY'S has been rated the best place to dine alone!

A favorite pastime in Ventura is to browse downtown's antique stores.

* * * * * * *

66 CALIFORNIA

Local Venturans and visitors have been eating out AND cooking it themselves for the past seven years at the 66 CALIFORNIA restaurant. Energetic patrons can rustle up their own steak and chicken on the large indoor grill and indulge in delicious accompaniments such as beer recipe chili beans, hot baked potatoes with all the trimmings and warm crusty sourdough rolls.

Of course, you don't HAVE TO work for your meal at this Jazz and Supper Club! The experienced staff are glad to prepare and serve breakfast, lunch and dinner 7 days a week. Jose Salazar, the Kitchen Manager from the day the doors opened, has created many of the tempting meals on the menu. The morning omelets to the evening Seafood Pasta and Chicken Delfino are tried and true favorites. Jose makes a fresh batch of incredible Boston Clam Chowder every Friday and Saturday morning and the regular customers beat a path to the door for a bowl.

The small patio is ideal for indulging in the California fresh air and sunshine. Inside, the booths are comfortable and the walls are lined with oil paintings of local sights. An authentic red English telephone booth stands guard in the back of the restaurant.

66 CALIFORNIA is a popular haunt for Jazz buffs. The live entertainment draws a large crowd of local Venturans, joined by visitors who travel from as far as Santa Barbara and Los Angeles to see and hear the musicians perform.

* * * * * * *

Boston Clam Chowder

1 LB. ONIONS, CHOPPED
1 LB. CELERY, DICED
24 OZ. POTATOES, DICED
12 OZ. CARROTS, DICED
8 OZ. CLAM BASE
1 QUART WATER
2 #5 (51 OZ. EACH) CANS CHOPPED
   CLAMS
1 TBSP. BLACK PEPPER
1 TSP. WHITE PEPPER
1 TBSP. THYME
1 OZ. LEA & PERRINS WORCESTERSHIRE
   SAUCE
3 BAY LEAVES
ROUX (1 LB. FLOUR SLOWLY MIXED INTO
   1 LB. MELTED BUTTER)
4 QUARTS HEAVY CREAM
1/2 TSP. HICKORY SMOKE
1 LB. CHOPPED CRISPY BACON
1 TSP. TABASCO

Sauté onions, celery, potatoes and carrots in butter until 'al dente'.

Add clam base, water and clams. Stir in black and white peppers, thyme, Worcestershire sauce and bay leaves. Heat to a soft boil.

Add roux to desired thickness, stirring constantly. Mix in heavy cream.

Just before serving, add hickory smoke, bacon and Tabasco. Makes 5 gallons.

* * * * * * *

The 66 CALIFORNIA claims to have Ventura's best clam chowder - and they just may be right!

Seafood Pasta

6 SHRIMP
6 OZ. SCALLOPS
3 OZ. SNOW CRABMEAT
6 OZ. WHITEFISH
1/2 TSP. GARLIC, CHOPPED
SALT TO TASTE
BUTTER
2 CUPS HEAVY CREAM
1/2 CUP PARMESAN CHEESE, GRATED
6 TO 8 CHERRY TOMATOES, HALVED
10 TO 12 OZ. LINQUINI, COOKED 'AL
    DENTE'

In a large pan, sauté shrimp, scallops, crabmeat, whitefish and garlic in butter. Season to taste with salt. Set aside and keep warm.

In a saucepan, bring cream to a boil over medium heat. Add 1/4 cup of the parmesan cheese and stir until thickened and bubbling.

Add hot pasta to the sauce.

To serve, top pasta and sauce with cherry tomatoes, then seafood and sprinkle with remaining 1/4 cup of parmesan cheese.

Makes two very generous servings.

* * * * * * *

This recipe was developed by Jose Salazar. He suggests accompanying it with a crisp green salad and freshly baked sourdough bread.

Chicken Delfino

1 WHOLE CHICKEN BREAST
FLOUR
1 EGG, BEATEN
VEGETABLE OIL
1 MEDIUM ZUCCHINI
1 YELLOW (CROOKNECK) SQUASH
1 RED BELL PEPPER
BUTTER
1/4 TSP. GARLIC, CHOPPED
WHITE WINE TO TASTE

Coat chicken breast with flour and dip in beaten egg. Sauté in vegetable oil until cooked through and golden brown. Set aside and keep warm.

Dice zucchini, yellow squash and red bell pepper very small. Sauté vegetables in butter and garlic until cooked but still crisp. Season with wine to taste.

Serve chicken topped with sautéed vegetables. Accompany with pasta and sprinkle with freshly grated parmesan cheese.

Makes one hearty serving.

* * * * * * *

ROSARITO
BEACH CAFE

Downtown Ventura's ROSARITO BEACH CAFE features authentic regional Mexican cuisine. Fresh mesquite grilled seafood, meat entrees, local produce and fresh handmade tortillas are their claim to fame.

The restaurant began as a small cafe across from the San Buenaventura Mission. There it thrived for over five years before moving to it's present location, a little further up main street, to the former home of Earle Stanley Gardner, the creator and writer of 81 Perry Mason novels. It is complete with a heated patio dining area and a full bar featuring fine tequilas and wines. For almost two years dinner has been served in the Spanish decor of this comfortable restaurant.

Sandy Smith, the chef and creator of this eatery has finally consented to reveal his much sought after recipe for Pumpkin Flan.

A previous career in psychology and an obsession with fine Mexican food may be responsible for the success of Sandy Smith's ROSARITO BEACH CAFE.

* * * * * * *

Rosarito Beach Cafe's
Pumpkin Flan

1/2 CUP WATER
2 3/4 CUPS SUGAR
1/2 TSP. CINNAMON
1/8 TSP. GROUND CLOVES
1 CUP UNSEASONED CANNED PUMPKIN
5 EGGS
1 CUP HEAVY CREAM
3/4 CUP MILK
2 TSP. VANILLA

Whisk together 3/4 cup of the sugar, cinnamon, cloves, pumpkin, eggs, cream, milk and vanilla. Set aside.

Mix 1/2 cup water and the remaining 2 cups of sugar in a saucepan and cook over high heat until it caramelizes - it will turn a golden brown color.

Pour the caramel into 8 oz. baking dishes and allow to set for 3 or 4 minutes.

Stir flan mix once again and pour evenly into the baking cups.

Place cups on a rimmed baking sheet and pour in water to about 1/2 way up the side of each baking cup.

Bake in a 350 degree oven until flans are set (when you can shake them without a liquid-like center).

* * * * * * *

Mission San Buenaventura was founded in 1782 by Father Junipero Serra.

* * * * * * *

A WALK THROUGH TIME

As far back as 3500 years ago, the land that is today known as Ventura was inhabited by prehistoric native Americans. Artifacts such as a stone bowl dating back to 600 B.C., prove it.

Around 1500 A.D. the Chumash Indians greatly enjoyed life in a village called Mitz-kanakan (meaning 'place of the jaw'). Archaeologists have unearthed many artifacts from the rich soil at the site of the Albinger Archaeological Museum such as arrowheads, shell beads and pieces of baskets.

Father Serra founded the Ventura Mission in 1782 but the existing church was not completed until 1809. Artifacts from the Spanish period, (1782-1822) include pottery, glass beads and crucifixes. They are on display at the Ventura County Museum.

After the Mexican independence from Spain in 1821, they occupied this area on land obtained through grants, until 1847.

On January 6, 1847 the American flag was raised here, and after the Mexican-American war was over California became a state on Sept. 9, 1850. During this pioneer period Ventura's first drug store and a large saloon were established. Numerous bottles, glasses and buttons were found during the excavation of the Archaeological Museum site.

Beginning in 1866 the Chinese settled on Figueroa Street in a small community. From 1905 to the 1920's they fled here from their war-torn country but always hoped to return. They are credited with forming a fire brigade and helping all of Ventura fight fires. Old coins, opium pipes and china are a few of the artifacts recovered from their laundry and general store.

* * * * * * *

CLASSIC CARROT CAFE

The CLASSIC CARROT CAFE was established in the fall of 1971 by Dolores and Craig Woods, two artists with years of cooking experience. Their goal was to create a one of a kind eatery, preparing healthy food from scratch, using the freshest, most wholesome ingredients available. They have succeeded in doing just that.

Craig, a musician, and Dolores, an art major, have taken a small lunch counter with just a few tables to the present cozy restaurant. The indoor dining room is decorated with art on the walls and hand painted tiles on the tables. Years ago they were the first restaurant in Ventura to have an all-weather, heated garden patio. Today this secluded dining area is hidden from the main road.

It is Dolores and Craig's philosophy to serve wonderfully satisfying vegetarian meals that help keep you looking good and feeling great. Fresh vegetables, brown rice, whole grain breads, fresh fruit and tofu are emphasized for optimum health. Eggs, cheese, chicken and tuna do appear in breakfast specials, hot and cold sandwiches and tacos. Don't pass up their Famous Classic Carrot Cake!

The CLASSIC CARROT, your neighborhood cafe, provides quick friendly service seven days a week. They are committed to creating gourmet natural foods, from simple to scrumptious!

* * * * * * *

Broccoli Feta Pie

1 TBSP. OIL OR NO STICK COOKING SPRAY
2 ONIONS, FINELY CHOPPED
6 CLOVES GARLIC, MINCED
2 TSP. DRIED DILL WEED
1 TSP. MARJORAM
6 CUPS CHOPPED FRESH BROCCOLI, STEMS
  INCLUDED
1/2 TSP. SALT OR SALT FREE SUBSTITUTE
1/8 TSP. CAYENNE OR BLACK PEPPER
4 EGGS OR EGG BEATERS
2 CUPS CRUMBLED FETA CHEESE
1/2 CUP MINCED FRESH PARSLEY
10 PHYLLO LEAVES, THAWED
1 TBSP. SESAME OR SUNFLOWER SEEDS

Oil pan and sauté onions, garlic, dill and marjoram.
When onions begin to soften and brown, add broccoli,
salt and pepper. Sauté a few minutes more and remove
from heat when broccoli is still bright green and
slightly crunchy but cooked. Set aside.

In a large bowl, beat eggs and add feta cheese,
parsley and onion-broccoli sauté.

Lay defrosted Phyllo sheets flat on table and spray 6
sheets, one at a time with non-stick cooking spray and
layer in a greased springform pan.

Pour in filling. Spray remaining four phyllo sheets
one at a time and lay on on top of the other over the
filling. Roll edges of dough up to form a crust around
the pie's edge. Spray the top with non-stick cooking
spray and sprinkle with seeds.

Bake in a preheated 350 degree oven for 40 to 45
minutes until top is golden brown. Allow to set before
serving. Makes approximately 6 low fat servings.

* * * * * * *

TONY'S
STEAK & SEAFOOD

COCKTAILS & ENTERTAINMENT

TONY'S STEAK AND SEAFOOD has been serving fine Eastern choice aged beef and fresh fish in Ventura for 14 years. The family owned and operated restaurant offers an extensive thirty-eight item menu plus three or four daily Chef's Specials.

Executive Chef, Jorge Ramirez has been working at TONY'S since day one. His love of cooking began at an exclusive country club where his father was a chef. His insistence on perfection has earned TONY'S beef the vote of Best Steak in the county for the past 10 years. Last year, due to an attentive staff, TONY'S was also voted Best Service - Anywhere, Anytime, in the county, as well as Best Seafood.

Chef Jorge has unselfishly shared the recipe for his very own Apple Cashew Chicken baked in an Apricot Brandy Sauce. One taste of this exquisite dish is enough to convince anyone to become a fan of Chef Jorge's. One thing is for sure, no one leaves TONY'S hungry.

Tony himself entertains his guests every Friday and Saturday night by playing the sax in a duo or trio at the Jazz Piano Bar.

TONY'S STEAK & SEAFOOD restaurant maintains a large local following by dishing out first rate food and drink in an efficient, friendly manner. It will surely continue being a Ventura tradition for many years to come.

* * * * * * *

Tony's Special Potato Skins

3 LARGE BAKING POTATOES
4 CUPS CANOLA OIL
1 1/2 CUPS OF YOUR FAVORITE SALSA
1 CUP SHREDDED CHEDDAR CHEESE
1 CUP SHREDDED JACK CHEESE
2 TBSP. SOUR CREAM
1 TSP. FRESH CILANTRO
OLIVES FOR GARNISH

Bake potatoes in a 400 degree oven for 1 hour or until tender. Then increase oven temperature to 500 degrees and continue baking for another 30 minutes.

Remove potatoes from oven and allow to cool. Cut potatoes in half, lengthwise, and hollow out center, leaving enough potato in to hold skin.

Fry potato halves in hot canola oil until light brown. In a small saucepan, heat salsa.

Top potato skins with warmed salsa and Cheddar and jack cheese.

Bake in a 350 degree oven for 15 minutes.

To serve, top potato skins with sour cream and garnish with olives and cilantro.

* * * * * *

Apple Cashew Chicken
baked in an
Apricot Brandy Sauce

1/2 CUP DICED ONION
1 TSP. FRESH GARLIC, CHOPPED
5 OZ. BUTTER
3 OZ. WHITE WINE
2 CUPS CUBED SOURDOUGH BREAD
3 GRANNY SMITH APPLES, CUT INTO 1/4
   INCH CUBES
3/4 CUP CHOPPED CASHEWS
1 TSP. RUBBED DALMATIAN SAGE
1/4 TSP. BLACK PEPPER
1/2 TSP. SALT
2 SQUIRTS LEA & PERRINS WORCESTERSHIRE
   SAUCE
PINCH OF THYME
6 BONELESS, SKINLESS CHICKEN BREASTS,
   6 TO 8 OZ. EACH

Sauté onions and fresh chopped garlic in butter until onions are translucent. Add white wine and simmer for one minute.

Place cubed sourdough bread in a large mixing bowl and toss with onion and garlic sauté.

Next, add the apples, cashews, sage, pepper, salt, Worcestershire sauce and thyme. Mix well by hand.

Lightly pound chicken breasts and place 5 oz. of stuffing on each. Roll corners up and turn them over carefully. Brush with butter and garlic. Bake in a 350° oven for 30 to 45 minutes. Top with Apricot Brandy Sauce and bake for an additional 5 minutes.

* * * * * * *

Apricot Brandy Sauce

2 CANS (TOTAL 32 OZ.) APRICOT HALVES
2 OZ. APRICOT BRANDY
1 CUP BROWN SUGAR
1 TSP. FRESH CHOPPED PARSLEY
2 OZ. HONEY
1 TBSP. CORNSTARCH MIXED WITH
   LUKEWARM WATER

Place all apricot halves and 1/2 of the juice in a blender and process.

Pour sauce into a saucepan. Add apricot brandy, brown sugar, parsley and honey.

Bring sauce almost to a boil and add cornstarch and water mixture slowly while whipping constantly.

Simmer for approximately 20 minutes.

Pour sauce over stuffed, baked Apple Cashew Chicken and bake for an additional 5 minutes.

This Apple Cashew Chicken baked in an Apricot Brandy recipe serves six.

* * * * * * *

Chef Jorge Ramirez created this dish and it has been a favorite at TONY'S for the past six years.

SEAFARER'S RESTAURANT

HOLIDAY INN

VENTURA BEACH RESORT

This towering landmark hotel on the Ventura coastline has long been the destination of seaside vacation seekers. The Ventura Beach Resort is a newly renovated, 12 story hotel featuring 260 luxurious guest rooms, 18 suites, and enough banquet space to accommodate 1200 guests.

The first floor lobby is filled with glistening chandeliers and poster size photos of Ventura's most interesting historical events. This is also where the local action can be found. Music and dance lovers frequent the Breakers Lounge for live entertainment on Friday and Saturday evenings. The Seafarer's Restaurant is the main dining hall with traditional fare served morning, noon and night.

The Top of the Harbor is an award winning, revolving, roof-top restaurant with a magnificent panoramic view of Ventura's mountains, the city and the Pacific Ocean. The evening sunsets are breathtaking. Innovative chefs out-do themselves to pamper the public with the Champagne Sunday Brunch. "Very Special Events" such as live comedy shows with Jimmie Walker and Bruce Baum are popular. For intimate conversation and a cocktail enjoy the view from the quiet Bayview Lounge.

The HOLIDAY INN VENTURA BEACH RESORT is just steps from the sand and a short walk to historic downtown Ventura. The dedicated staff welcomes visitors and locals to discover a variety of dining and entertainment pleasures. Satisfaction is guaranteed!

* * * * * * *

Caldo Verde

1 MEDIUM ONION
1 LB. PEELED POTATOES
4 CUPS WATER
1 TBSP. CHICKEN BASE
1/2 TSP. BLACK PEPPER
ROUX TO THICKEN
1 TBSP. OLIVE OIL
5 OZ. LINQUISA SAUSAGE
2 CUPS FRESH KALE

Thinly slice onions and potatoes. Place in a large stock pot and cover with 4 cups water. Mix in 1 Tbsp. chicken base and 1/2 Tbsp. black pepper.

Bring to a boil and cook until the onions and potatoes soften and soup begins to thicken.

While soup is cooking, heat olive oil in a sauté pan and cook linquisa sausage until well done. Dice into small pieces and add both the sausage and juices from the pan into the soup.

If necessary, add roux (1 Tbsp. flour mixed with 2 Tbsp. melted butter) to thicken soup.

Just before serving, stir 2 cups of thinly shredded kale into the Caldo Verde. Serve hot.

* * * * * * *

Caldo Verde means Green Soup. This delicious soup is a native Portuguese dish and is served in every restaurant in Portugal.

The Ventura Pier, a historical landmark, is California's longest wooden pier - 1958 feet long.

* * * * * * *

THE HISTORIC
VENTURA PIER

San Buenaventura is the proud owner of California's longest wooden pier. This recreational attraction is now coveted by fisherman and daily visitors, some out for a leisurely stroll to bask in the warm California sun and enjoy the cool ocean breezes, some jogging for fitness. The beautiful pier is a sturdy, newly renovated structure; but it wasn't always so.

More than 100 years ago, before 1873, Venturans inhabited a sleepy little town nestled between the mountains and the Pacific Ocean. All that changed when the 1200 foot long San Buenaventura Wharf was built. It served to accommodate cargo ships while they loaded and unloaded lumber, oil and grains. Time and Mother Nature both took their toll on the pier. In 1914 huge waves forced a ship docked along side the wharf to crash into it, splitting it in half. It was repaired and extended to 1700 feet in 1917, only to have over 1000 feet once again demolished by the sea in 1937.

Unable to do without the majestic landmark, Venturans rebuilt and extended it to 1958 feet the next year. Since then it has been used for pleasure only. All was well until 1986 when a fierce storm destroyed one third of the pier. Not until the historical landmark underwent a major restoration (including a massive, bronze water sculpture, 'Wavespout') and reopened in October 1993 were visitors and locals able to fully enjoy one of Ventura's most prized possessions.

These days, from sunup to sundown, there is nothing more relaxing and refreshing than a stroll along the historic Ventura Pier.

* * * * * * *

53

ERIC ERICSSON'S FISH COMPANY

"SEAFOOD PREPARED TO ITS BEST"

ERIC ERICSSON'S has been "Ventura's Seafood Tradition since 1981". They have very cleverly incorporated seafood into a variety of ethnic dishes and have succeeded in creating a menu that has something for everyone.

The restaurant located "Where Seaward Meets The Sea" always uses as many fresh ingredients as possible to make such dishes as Seafood Marinara, Shellfish Pesto, Viking Chowder, Grilled Eggplant and Shrimp, a Shrimp and Crab Quesadilla and Spicy Indonesian Peanut Sauce with Chicken or Shrimp. For the meat and potato lovers, steak, pork chops, chicken and burgers are prepared.

Delicious homemade desserts have caused the Los Angeles Times to consider "ERIC ERICSSON'S The Dessert Haven of Ventura and Beyond Seafood".

Patrons may relax in the cozy bar room apart from the main dining room. On Saturday and Sunday, after dinner there is no need to get back in the car to look for entertainment. Adjacent to the restaurant is ERIC ERICSSON'S CLUB. They feature live music with an emphasis on Caribbean pop (reggae) and blues.

Whenever seeking seafood with a twist sail on to ERIC ERICSSON'S - ON THE BEACH!

* * * * * * *

Fresh
Mango Papaya Kiwi
Salsa

2 FRESH MANGOS
2 FRESH PAPAYAS
2 FRESH KIWIS
1 BUNCH FRESH CILANTRO
FRESH SERRANO CHILI, TO TASTE
FRESH LIME JUICE, TO TASTE
DASH SALT

Peel fruit. Coarsely chop mangos, papayas, kiwis, cilantro and chili. Add dash of salt and toss with fresh lime juice. Garnish with cilantro sprigs.

This versatile salsa may be refrigerated for several days. It is deliciously refreshing served with grilled fish or shrimp.

* * * * * * *

A Serrano is a small (1 1/2 inch long) hot green chili pepper. It is available canned or fresh. If a milder flavor is desired, remove the seeds of the chili. If canned, rinse under cold water as most of the heat is in the liquid.

THE GALLERY RESTAURANT
DOUBLETREE HOTEL VENTURA

The DOUBLETREE HOTEL VENTURA, one of 85 Doubletree Hotels and Canadian Pacific Hotels and Resorts in North America is home to THE GALLERY RESTAURANT. It is uniquely decorated with an ever changing display of paintings (all available for purchase) furnished by the California Gold Coast Water Color Society. Originally founded in 1990 by 8 local artists to promote excellence in watercolor paintings, the society now boasts over 150 members.

The DOUBLETREE HOTEL VENTURA is located, conveniently, just a short walk from the beach. The lush greenery and numerous cascading waterfalls in the hotel lobby and courtyard are an enticement to sit and relax a while, to take life a little slower. The popular C.J. Nelson's sportsbar draws a fun-loving crowd by featuring satellite sports coverage, nightly drink specials, Bullpen appetizers and live bands on Friday and Saturday nights.

The GALLERY RESTAURANT proudly serves fresh local fish and fresh locally grown fruits and vegetables, all with a Southwestern flavor. Daily Chef's specials and gourmet desserts in addition to their new Twilight Dinners, Prime Rib Buffet on Friday and Saturday evenings and the Sunday Champagne Brunch capture the taste buds of local Venturans and visitors.

THE GALLERY RESTAURANT and DOUBLETREE HOTEL VENTURA are very community oriented. Their high social awareness ranges from actively conserving our most precious resource, water, recycling waste products, and supporting the Ventura County Special Olympics.

* * * * * * *

56

Medallions of Salmon sautéed with Zinfandel Butter

1/4 CUP BUTTER OR MARGARINE
1/4 LB. MUSHROOMS (LOCAL, SLICED THIN)
3/4 LB. BONELESS, SKINLESS SALMON
  FILET (CUT IN 6 EQUAL PIECES)
2 TBSP. FINELY DICED SHALLOTS
2/3 CUP ZINFANDEL WINE (YOUR LOCAL
  FAVORITE)
CHIVES (FINELY CUT)

Melt 1 Tbsp. of the butter in a 12 inch sauté pan over medium heat. Add sliced and washed mushrooms and sauté until lightly browned, about 6 to 9 minutes. Remove from pan, set aside and keep warm.

Add 1 more Tbsp. of the butter to same pan and melt. Add salmon medallions to pan, season lightly with salt and pepper and sauté until lightly browned, firm and translucent at the thickest part (open or cut to test), about 7 to 10 minutes total. Remove from pan and keep warm.

In the same sauté pan, combine shallots and Zinfandel. Bring to a boil uncovered until mixture is reduced to about 1/4 cup - about 4 minutes. Reduce heat to low. Add remaining 2 Tbsp. soft butter, little by little, until melted and sauce is smooth.

Place salmon medallions on dinner plates. Top with mushrooms, spoon sauce over and garnish with chives. Accompany with fresh local asparagus and carrots. Serves two.

* * * * * * *

Sea Bass Encrusted with Pistachios and Coconut served with Grilled Manzana Bananas and a Citrus Avocado Honey Glaze

1 LB. BONELESS, SKINLESS SEA BASS FILETS
  (CUT INTO FOUR PORTIONS)
SALT AND WHITE PEPPER
ALL-PURPOSE FLOUR
1/2 CUP CRUSHED PISTACHIO NUTS
1/2 CUP FINELY GRATED COCONUT
1 EGG (BEATEN WITH 2 TBSP. MILK)
1/4 CUP CANOLA OIL OR OTHER NON-
  CHOLESTEROL OIL
3 MANZANA BANANAS (PEELED AND CUT
  LENGTHWISE)
JUICE FROM ONE ORANGE
LOCAL AVOCADO HONEY TO TASTE
1 TSP. ARROWROOT OR CORNSTARCH

Rinse fish and pat dry. Lightly salt and pepper. Dust lightly with flour, dip fish into egg mixture, drain briefly, then coat with a mixture of pistachios and coconut.

Sauté filets until golden brown in hot canola oil, turn and cook until done at the thickest point (open fish and test) for 6 to 10 minutes. Remove from pan, keep warm.

Lightly flour bananas and grill in canola oil until golden brown on both sides.

FOR GLAZE - Bring orange juice to a boil and add honey to taste. Stir in a small amount of arrowroot or cornstarch and water mixture while constantly whisking until sauce is slightly thick.

Arrange the sea bass filets and Manzana bananas on a warm plate with your favorite fresh local vegetables and steamed basmati rice. Spoon glaze over fish and bananas. Serves two.

* * * * * * *

This delicious recipe features locally caught sea bass paired with Manzana bananas grown just a few miles up the coast, near Carpenteria. The citrus is also native to Ventura, as is the avocado honey.

Chef Gil Scorse created this recipe and the Medallions of Salmon with Zinfandel Butter. He has been successfully overseeing the operations of the GALLERY RESTAURANT for six of its eight years.

The Ventura Harbor Village is an ideal place to enjoy waterfront dining and stroll the promenade.

* * * * * * *

VENTURA HARBOR

Ventura's pride and joy is a picturesque harbor made up of 1500 boat slips, 2 yacht clubs, the Channel Islands National Park Visitors Center and a quaint mediterranean-style seaside village. A wide variety of year-round activities promise endless entertainment for all ages.

The star attraction is the Ventura Harbor Village, a haven for shoppers and diners, with over 40 specialty shops, gourmet restaurants and casual bistros. Diners may choose from ice cream or cappuccino, burgers and fries, or fresh fish and fine Italian cuisine. Most restaurants, like Frullati's Cafe Della Riviera, offer patio dining with fabulous harbor views. Children love to ride the handpainted carousel and a small group of musicians can usually be found performing an open air concert on the weekends. Evening entertainment at the Comedy Club and the Theatre by the Sea is popular.

Water sports are a favorite California coast pastime. Scuba diving lessons and rentals, along with surfboards, bodyboards, canoes, sailboats and paddle boats are available. There are several charter boats for deep sea fishing, whale watching tours and day trips to any of the five Channel Islands.

The harbor is the home of annual events such as the Fiesta del Sol (celebration of the sun), the Christmas Parade of Lights, the Ventura Channel Dash (speedboats), and the Ventura Cup (yachts).

Land lovers will find the adjacent beach is ideal for sunbathing, family picnics or fishing along the jetties.

Discover beautiful Ventura Harbor. The memories will last a lifetime.

* * * * * * *

FRULLATI'S
CAFE DELLA RIVIERA

The CAFE DELLA RIVIERA is the creation of Fabrizo and Elizabeth, true entrepreneurs with a passion for perfection. This Italian restaurant, in the Ventura Harbor Village is filled with nautical touches, such as the beautiful boat (handmade by Fabrizio), suspended upside-down from the ceiling. The built-in wine racks display a fine collection for connoisseurs to savor.

This charming bistro is enhanced by the alfresco dining on the patio. The warm sunshine and cool breeze coupled with the pictorial harbor view is pure California dreaming.

And the food is to die for! There is a wide range of traditional Italian specialties on the menu, although the emphasis is on the rich butter and cream sauces of Northern Italy. Full breakfast on the weekend, classic sandwiches on fresh breads, homemade soups and crisp salads for lunch, and gourmet Italian dinner entrees such as Veal Marsala are all prepared to satisfy the most demanding of critics. But the star of the show is the fresh pasta creations and their sumptuous sauces, cooked to order in individual sauté pans in under 10 minutes. There are always several specials on the board that combine seafood with the pasta. The Spaghettini with Lobster in a light tomato basil sauce and Fettuccini Alfredo with Salmon are out of this world. Finish with a heavenly cappuccino.

Mouthwatering Italian food and Fabrizo's attention to every detail is what makes FRULLATI'S CAFE DELLA RIVIERA the best thing to happen to the Ventura Harbor Village.

* * * * * * *

Chicken Alfredo

4 OZ. SPAGHETTI
BUTTER AND OLIVE OIL
1 BONELESS, SKINLESS CHICKEN BREAST,
   CUT INTO STRIPS
FRESH CHOPPED GARLIC, TO TASTE
3/4 CUP WHIPPING CREAM
PINCH WHITE PEPPER
1/2 CUP PARMESAN CHEESE, GRATED
FRESH PARSLEY, CHOPPED, FOR GARNISH

Bring a large pot of salted water (like the Mediterranean Sea!) to a full boil and add the 4 oz. of pasta. Boil for 7 to 8 minutes, stirring occasionally, until 'al dente'.

Meanwhile, melt butter and oil in a 10 inch skillet and sauté chicken strips until cooked through. Add garlic and sauté until lightly browned. May add a little white wine, if desired.

Stir in the whipping cream and pinch white pepper. Allow the sauce to simmer and continue cooking until it has reduced in volume and thickened slightly.

Gently stir in drained, hot spaghetti and grated parmesan cheese. Mix well. If the alfredo sauce is not of the proper consistency, add more parmesan cheese to thicken or a little more cream to dilute.

Serve hot, garnished with chopped parsley. Makes one generous serving.

* * * * * * *

This delicious gourmet meal takes only 10 minutes to prepare at home. If using fresh pasta, as the CAFE DELLA RIVIERA does, the cooking time is only 7 to 8 minutes.

ALEXANDER'S DINING AND DANCING

COLONY HARBORTOWN MARINA RESORT

Look no further for exceptional service and food. ALEXANDER'S restaurant, in the Colony Harbortown Marina Resort, gladly provides both.

Lunch selections include an array of gourmet appetizers such as Brie and Papaya Quesadillas. Favorite conventional sandwiches and fresh salads are wonderful, but the talk of the town is their toss-your-own Caesar Salad and incredible Pasta Bar. This dish is created right before your eyes from a large selection of fresh ingredients expertly sautéed by a chef whose aim is to please.

Dinner offers many of the same delicious choices plus such delectable entrées as Ventura Steak (New York steak stuffed with green chilies) and Lobster Ravoli. Easy listening music is piped in overhead, the atmosphere is relaxed and the service is exceptional. Their "Toast of the Gold Coast Champagne Sunday Brunch" should not be missed.

ALEXANDER'S large entertainment room hosts a comfortable bar and live music, just right for dancing one's cares away. Top 40 tunes, the piano bar, jazz and blues, and Tropical Nights (with free dance lessons) are all very popular evening attractions.

The Harbortown Resort is an ideal vacation spot for a romantic get-a-way, a family holiday or any size business conference. This beautiful complex is famous for luring visitors from the stifling heat and city smog to the clean, fresh air of Ventura.

* * * * * * *

New York Peppersteak

10 OZ. NEW YORK STEAK
1/2 TSP. CRACKED BLACK PEPPER
1/2 OZ. CLARIFIED BUTTER
1 TSP. SHALLOTS
2 OZ. BURGUNDY WINE
1/2 TSP. GREEN PEPPERCORNS
3 OZ. BROWN SAUCE
1 TSP. SOUR CREAM

Dust New York steak with cracked black pepper. Melt butter in a skillet and sauté steak over a low flame.

Meanwhile, place shallots, Burgundy wine, green peppercorns and brown sauce in a bowl and mix.

Add mixture to the steak in the sauté pan and stir in sour cream. Continue cooking for 5 minutes.

Serve immediately. Makes one generous portion.

* * * * * *

The Channel Islands Visitor Center at the tip of the Ventura Harbor is the gateway to the islands.

* * * * * * *

66

A FLOATING WILDLIFE PRESERVE

One of California's best kept secrets is the Channel Islands National Park, 5 tranquil islands in a 250,000 acre wilderness preserve, several miles off Ventura's coast. A few of the activities enjoyed by visitors are camping, hiking, picnicking, scuba diving, seal and sea lion viewing, swimming, tidepooling and whale watching.

Each island is unique. The Santa Rosa Island is where the Old West lives on. It's ranching days began 140 years ago and continue today. After spending 2 years grazing on the island, cattle weighing 1,000 pounds each are ferried some 40 miles across the Channel in a floating cattle pen to the mainland. San Miguel Island is the breeding ground to over 70,000 California sea lions, 50,000 northern elephant seals and 5,000 northern fur seals. On Anacapa Island, the visitors center features an Underwater Video Program displaying some of the 1,000 species of plants and animals in the kelp forest. The island's historic lighthouse, built in 1932, has been converted to solar power. Santa Barbara Island features 6 miles of scenic hiking trails and is a bird watchers paradise. The 60,000 acres of Santa Cruz Island are inhabited by over 600 plant species, 140 types of land birds and many nesting sea birds.

The ideal place to explore all the interesting features the islands have to offer is the Channel Islands National Park Visitor Center at the tip of the Ventura Harbor. Their tidepool is filled with sea creatures and the observation tower provides a panoramic 360 degree view of both land and water. They gladly help fascinated visitors to decide which island trip may best suit their needs.

* * * * * * *

GARFIELDS
BAR & GRILL

PARTY ALL WEEKEND!

GARFIELDS BAR & GRILL has become a Ventura institution over the past 12 years. This midtown eatery sports a full bar with Beer Bucket Specials and Saturday Bloody Mary Mornings. The laid back attitude of the down-home bar even encourages tossing peanut shells on the floor!

The pub's customers can sit there for hours, just relaxing and taking in the most unusual decor, and still not see it all. Surfboards and fake sharks wearing baseball caps hang from the ceiling, old photos and drawings (most with a little character added to them - probably by a customer), antique license plates and lots more memorabilia decorate the walls.

If that's not entertaining enough, there are so many TV's that one can be seen from every seat in the house. Their motto is PARTY ALL WEEKEND! (And that's why they need Bloody Mary Mornings!) Live bands with names like Nasty Jack and Ju Ju Eyeball perform most Friday and Saturday nights.

GARFIELDS is a great casual lunch or dinner spot that boasts of flipping the "Best Burgers in Town!" They are also home of GARFIELDS' Famous Peel 'N Eat Shrimp, a shellfish lovers delight!

For a cold brew and a bite to eat, head over to GARFIELDS.

* * * * * * *

Garfields' Famous
Peel 'N Eat Shrimp

1 LB. (16/21) FROZEN, HEADLESS SHRIMP
GARFIELDS' COCKTAIL SAUCE

Thaw the shrimp. (The term 16/21 refers to the size of the shrimp; there are 16 to 21 shrimp in each pound.)

Bring equal parts beer and water to a full boil in a large pot. Add thawed shrimp for exactly 3 minutes.

This cooking time is critical for obtaining perfectly cooked shrimp.

Drain shrimp and chill by immediately covering with ice. The shrimp should have a crisp consistency.

Serve with fresh lemon slices and GARFIELDS' cocktail sauce.

GARFIELDS' COCKTAIL SAUCE

9/10 GALLON KETCHUP
1 CUP HORSERADISH
4 TSP. LEMON JUICE
2 TSP. WORCESTERSHIRE SAUCE

Combine all ingredients well. Makes 1 gallon cocktail sauce.

Serve with Peel 'N Eat Shrimp.

* * * * * * *

ELEPHANT

BAR & RESTAURANT

The ELEPHANT BAR is home to the Coco Loco, a delicious drink made from a secret combination of tropical juices and liqueurs that they claim will make your trunk tingle! Customers may relax on the open air patio with a selection from the full bar or a specialty drink (full strength or non-alcoholic). A classic favorite is the Big E Combo, a smooth 23 oz. ale and a Big E Burger.

Casual meals in the restaurant are chosen from huge, brightly colored menus. Sandwiches, burgers and pasta dishes are created with a fresh California flair. With the best health in mind, only canola oil is used for frying.

The family oriented ELEPHANT BAR employs friendly servers who happily help keep children entertained by providing them with their own special menu sporting wild animals to color, crayons in an elephants foot and balloons.

Whole herds of local Venturans have been stampeding to the ELEPHANT BAR for the past decade. The restaurant features a jungle theme, from the rows of synchronized mobile fans on the ceilings of the bar, handpainted tropical birds on the walls, comfy rattan furniture in the lounge and the forest green carpet on the floor.

So the next time you are searching for a wild idea, hike on over to the ELEPHANT BAR & RESTAURANT for some tropical treats.

* * * * * * *

California Artichoke Spinach Dip

4 OZ. BUTTER, SOFTENED
6 OZ. YELLOW SPANISH ONION, 1/4" DICE
1 1/2 TBSP. FRESH GARLIC, CHOPPED
1 1/2 OZ. ALL-PURPOSE FLOUR
5 OZ. ARTICHOKE JUICE, RESERVED
    FROM CANNED ARTICHOKES
1/2 CUP CHABLIS WINE
2 OZ. CREAM
8 OZ. PEPPER JACK CHEESE, GRATED
3 OZ. PARMESAN CHEESE, GRATED
10 OZ. FRESH SPINACH, WASHED, WELL
    DRAINED, NO EXCESS STEM, CHOPPED
    INTO 1/4 IN PIECES
10 TO 12 OZ. ARTICHOKE HEART QUARTERS
    WELL DRAINED, COARSELY CHOPPED
1 TSP. LEA & PERRINS WORCESTERSHIRE
    SAUCE
1 TSP. COLMAN'S GROUND DRY MUSTARD

Melt butter in a heavy braising pan over medium heat.
Do not brown. Add onions and garlic and cook, stirring
occasionally, until the onions are tender.

Add flour using a wire whip to blend all ingredients
together. Continue cooking for 4 to 5 minutes, stirring
occasionally to ensure uniform heating.

Add the reserved artichoke juice, wine and cream
slowly while whipping vigorously with the wire whip
to prevent lumping. Stirring constantly to prevent
sticking, allow the base to come to a full, rolling boil.
Lower heat and simmer base for 3 minutes.

Slowly add the cheeses, being sure each addition of
cheese is completely melted before adding more.
Remove from heat and pour into a large bowl. Add
remaining ingredients and mix very well. Serve with
corn tortilla chips or bagel chips.

* * * * * * *

FLAVOR OF INDIA

FINE INDIAN CUISINE

The FLAVOR OF INDIA was such a huge success in Santa Barbara that owners, Kuldip (Sam) and Dropati (Patty) Samra were inspired to open a second restaurant and introduce the City of Ventura to their authentic cuisine. Open since 1993 at this location, they are doing a fine job of tempting the public with Indian delicacies.

An education into the Indian style of cooking begins with the first glance at the menu. An appetizer to sample is a Samosa, an Indian pastry stuffed with mildly spiced mashed potatoes and peas, or lamb and peas. Lentils are an important dietary staple and are found in many traditional dishes. It is soon apparent that curry and garam masala are popular spices used in cooking. When ordering, Sam requests that mild, medium or a spicy touch be specified. Meats are cooked until tender in a Tandoor, an Indian oven which is a 5000 year old tradition. There is a meal to suit everyone's palate including chicken, lamb, shrimp and many vegetarian delights.

No look into this fascinating culture would be complete without tasting a Biryanis (an aromatic basmati rice) dish. The same for the freshly baked Tandoori breads. Chapati is made from whole wheat flour and Naan is the popular Indian style pastry flour bread.

From the moment the door of FLAVOR OF INDIA is opened, the sounds and scents of the Indian culture warmly embrace each guest and the journey to a faraway place begins.

* * * * * * *

Mixed Vegetables of India

1 TBSP. VEGETABLE OIL
1 MEDIUM ONION, CHOPPED
2 TSP. GINGER, CHOPPED
2 TSP. GARLIC, CHOPPED
2 MEDIUM TOMATOES, CHOPPED
1 TSP. RED PEPPER
1 TSP. PAPRIKA
1 TSP. TURMERIC
2 TSP. GARAM MASALA
SALT TO TASTE
1/2 LB. CARROTS, CHOPPED
1/2 LB. POTATOES, CHOPPED
1/4 LB. MUSHROOMS, CHOPPED
1/4 LB. PEAS
1/2 LB. CAULIFLOWER, CHOPPED

Heat vegetable oil in a large frying pan. Sauté chopped onion until lightly browned.

Mix in ginger and garlic with onions and sauté for 5 minutes.

Add chopped tomatoes, red pepper, paprika, turmeric, garam masala and salt to taste. Cook for an additional 5 minutes.

Stir in chopped carrots and cook for 7 to 10 minutes.

Mix in potatoes, mushrooms, peas and cauliflower and cook until the vegetables are tender.

Serve hot with Chapatis, Indian Bread.

* * * * * * *

The spice, garam masala, may be found in Indian food shops.

Lamb Curry

1 TBSP. VEGETABLE OIL
4 MEDIUM ONIONS, CHOPPED
2 OZ. GINGER, CHOPPED
2 OZ. GARLIC, CHOPPED
4 TOMATOES, CHOPPED
1 TSP. RED PEPPER
1 TSP. PAPRIKA
SALT TO TASTE
1 TBSP. TURMERIC
2 TBSP. GARAM MASALA
2 LBS. LAMB, CUT IN CHUNKS

Heat vegetable oil in a large sauté pan. Sauté chopped onions until lightly browned.

Add ginger and garlic and continue cooking for 5 minutes.

Stir in chopped tomatoes, red pepper, paprika, salt to taste, turmeric and garam masala. Mix well and cook for an additional 5 to 10 minutes.

Add lamb chunks and 1/2 cup of water and mix well.

Continue to cook until lamb is tender.

Serve with hot rice.

* * * * * * *

EXPLORE OXNARD!

The City of Oxnard, home of the California Strawberry Festival, is a diverse arena of never-ending entertainment opportunities. From fascinating museums and the historic Heritage Square to the Channel Islands Harbor, residents and visitors can always find something interesting to do!

Channel Islands Harbor has been described as "one of the fastest growing resort areas between Los Angeles and San Francisco". The area is filled with communities of beautiful new homes built at the waters edge, some with boat docks at their back door. Fabulous get-a-way sites such as Casa Sirena Marina Resort and Mandalay Beach Resort are favorite vacation destinations for stressed city dwellers looking to escape the heat and smog.

The Harbor is home to two villages. Fisherman's Wharf, a shopping courtyard with New England-style architecture, is where the Ventura County Maritime Museum exhibits sea treasures. Harbor Landing, famous for it's array of fabulous dining pleasures, is surrounded by a promenade ideal for walking or bicycling. A variety of events, such as the Channel Islands Food and Wine Festival, draw large crowds.

The weekly Farmer's Market is a popular spot for Mexican food, live entertainment and a vast supply of fresh produce from rich farmlands. Strawberries and lemons are the county's top money making crops. A weekly antique street fair is a favorite pastime. Children of all ages love the hands-on Gull Wings Children's Museum.

Whether exploring the Channel Islands Harbor, visiting Heritage Square, or attending a local festival, Oxnard has something for everyone.

* * * * * * *

BARBI'S
BAKERY

"ADDICTIVE SINCE 1984"

BARBI'S claim, "ADDICTIVE SINCE 1984" is not just nonchalant bragging. It's the absolute truth! It is doubtful that anyone has made just one trip to BARBI'S BAKERY in the Channel Islands Harbor.

If the aroma of freshly brewed gourmet coffee isn't enough, the sight of all those cheesecakes, muffins, layer cakes, cookies, brownies and giant cinnamon rolls will surely get you in the door.

Once inside the long, narrow bakery and coffee bar, it is impossible to escape without eating at least one of BARBI'S incredible creations. On any given day customers will drool over 20 of the 35 different kinds of muffins she makes fresh, from scratch. It is the same with the cheesecakes; one may be lucky enough to sample Cappuccino, Chocolate Chip Cookie Crunch, Jack Daniels and Raisin, Peanut Butter Fudge, Pineapple Macadamia or any other of the 36 flavors that she whips up. She also makes specialty cakes for any occasion.

Barbi Kurisu has been tempting the Ventura area for 10 years now, the last 4 of those at this location. The brightly decorated coffee shop displays a collection of coffee pots, some antiques, some just unusual.

Locals and area visitors can satisfy sweet cravings at BARBI'S BAKERY then stroll around the harbor and enjoy the fresh air.

* * * * * * *

Carrot or Zucchini Muffins

4 CUPS FLOUR
1 CUP SUGAR
1 CUP BROWN SUGAR
2 TSP. BAKING POWDER
2 TSP. BAKING SODA
1/4 TSP. NUTMEG
2 TSP. CINNAMON
1/4 TSP. GINGER
1 TSP. SALT
1/3 CUP OIL
4 EGGS
2 CUPS SHREDDED CARROTS OR ZUCCHINI
1 CUP WALNUTS
2 TSP. VANILLA
16 OZ. CRUSHED PINEAPPLE
1/2 CUP RAISINS

Mix all the dry ingredients together in a large bowl.

Slowly add the wet ingredients. Mix briefly.

Pour into muffin pans.

Bake in a preheated 350 degree oven for 25 to 30 minutes.

* * * * * * *

Barbi's Classic Cheesecake

FILLING:
 2 LBS. CREAM CHEESE
 1 1/4 CUPS SUGAR
 5 WHOLE EGGS
 1 TBSP. FRESH LEMON JUICE
 2 TSP. PURE VANILLA

CRUST:
 2 CUPS GRAHAM CRACKER CRUMBS
 1/2 CUP GROUND VANILLA WAFERS
 1/4 CUP GROUND WALNUTS (OPTIONAL)
 1/4 CUP, PLUS A LITTLE, MELTED BUTTER
 1/4 CUP SUGAR

TOPPING:
 2 CUPS SOUR CREAM
 1/4 CUP SUGAR
 1 TSP. VANILLA

FOR FILLING: Beat cream cheese until smooth. Slowly add sugar and beat until smooth. Add eggs slowly, one at a time, then add lemon juice and vanilla. Beat on medium speed for 5 minutes until smooth.

FOR CRUST: Mix ingredients together by hand and press into the bottom and sides of a springform pan.

Pour batter into crust and bake in a 350 degree oven for 55 minutes. Keeping the oven door closed, turn oven off and allow cheesecake to cool in the oven for an additional 30 minutes. Don't open the oven door during baking or cooling period.

FOR TOPPING: Mix all ingredients together by hand and pour onto cake. Bake to set for 7 minutes in 350° oven. Cool for at least 8 hours in refrigerator.

* * * * * * *

Barbi's Classic Cheesecake II

SUGARFREE & LOWER IN FAT, TOO!

To accommodate all of her customers needs, Barbi has devised a sugarfree and a reduced fat version of her famous cheesecake. Simply follow the recipe for the Classic Cheesecake, making the substitutions outlined below.

FOR FILLING: Omit the sugar from the original recipe and substitute 1 cup of fresh fruit puree or applesauce.

Substitute 10 egg whites for the 5 whole eggs in the filling.

FOR CRUST: Omit the sugar and nuts from the original recipe.

FOR TOPPING: Omit the sugar and substitute a dietetic sweetener.

FOLLOW ALL OTHER DIRECTIONS AS GIVEN.

Serves 16.

* * * * * * *

CHUY'S
&
KONA RANCH HOUSE

It is easy to find the best of both worlds in the Channel Islands Harbor. CHUY'S and the KONA RANCH HOUSE are conveniently located under one roof.

Just inside the front door, to the right, is a surfers dream, a real California beach bar! It is complete with a huge shark suspended from the ceiling, brightly painted walls, a green bar and of course, a pool table. The casual atmosphere extends outside to the patio where customers can relax and watch the boats sail by in the harbor.

To eat in or take out, there is plenty to snack on from CHUY'S, the home of affordable mesquite grilled chicken, tri-tip and fish, with all the fixings. For the past 4 years hungry folks have dug into the Mexican style meals that come with lots of rice, beans and tortillas.

The KONA RANCH HOUSE occupies the same building but seems as though it is miles away. The quiet, upscale restaurant offers a harbor view from every table, impeccable service and the same fabulous mesquite grilled tender dishes as CHUY'S. Plus choice steaks, prime rib, seafood, salad bar and freshly made desserts from Barbi's Bakery.

The uniqueness of two restaurants in one, high quality food and the teamwork of it's employees is responsible for the success of CHUY'S & KONA RANCH HOUSE.

* * * * * * *

Kona Roll-Ups

1 MEDIUM LARGE FLOUR TORTILLA
2 OZ. CREAM CHEESE
1/4 TSP. OLD BAY SEASONING
1 1/2 OZ. DRY PICO (CHOPPED TOMATO,
    ONION AND CILANTRO)
1 OZ. CELERY, CHOPPED
1/2 OZ. BLACK OLIVES, CHOPPED
1/2 OZ. FRESH SPINACH, CHOPPED
2 OZ. COOKED CHICKEN, DICED OR 2 OZ.
    COOKED CRABMEAT AND SHRIMP
2 OZ. TACO SAUCE OR RANCH DRESSING

Lightly grill tortilla on each side.

Spread tortilla with cream cheese and dust with Old Bay Seasoning.

Sprinkle with Dry Pico, chopped celery, black olives and fresh spinach.

Add either 2 oz. of diced, cooked chicken or 2 oz. cooked crabmeat and shrimp combination.

Roll up gently and cut into 4 sections.

To serve, position around the edge of a plate and accompany with taco sauce or ranch dressing.

* * * * * * *

CHUY'S & KONA RANCH HOUSE were awarded Second Place for Decor in the 1994 Channel Islands Harbor Food and Wine Festival. They think it was for the girl in the hula skirt and coconut top!

Garlic Shrimp Sauce

4 LBS. BUTTER
1 1/2 CUPS CRUSHED CROUTONS
1 1/2 CUPS PALE SHERRY (NOT COOKING)
5 CUPS GARLIC, MINCED
4 CUPS GREEN ONIONS, FINELY DICED
3 CUPS FRESH BASIL, CHOPPED
3 CUPS TOMATOES, FINELY DICED
4 TSP. SALT
4 TSP. WHITE PEPPER
4 TSP. LEMON PEPPER

Allow butter to soften.

Add croutons and sherry. Blend well.

Stir in garlic, green onions, basil, tomatoes, salt, white pepper and lemon pepper. Blend very well.

To refrigerate or freeze, store in a tightly covered container.

Use 5 ounces per serving.

* * * * * * *

This recipe is probably too large for most families and can be reduced by decreasing the ingredients to the portion size desired.

Although this is a garlic sauce for shrimp, it is also excellent with other seafood and chicken.

Oxnard's Channel Islands Harbor is a popular resort and recreational area.

* * * * * * *

FILOMENA'S
ITALIAN KITCHEN

Filomena D'Amore is a second generation pizza expert. Her father, Patsy, came to New York directly from Naples, Italy in the 1920's. Patsy and his brother opened restaurants in Brooklyn and Boston before traveling west to introduce pizza to Hollywood.

When Patsy installed his pizza maker in the front window of his Casa D'Amore restaurant to entice the locals to try a slice of the homemade pie, he caught the attention of Frank Sinatra, who loved the friendly Italian and his pizza. The rest is history. Business was booming when Patsy met Rose, they married and opened an over the counter Pizzeria in the Los Angeles Farmers Market (still family owned and operated to this day). Then came the larger Villa Capri restaurant.

This was the meeting place of the stars. Marilyn Monroe and Joe DiMaggio were regulars. James Dean ate his last meal there before taking that fateful drive. Jackie Gleason, Jimmy Durante, Dean Martin, Bogie and Bocall, Sammy Davis Jr., Robert Wagner and Natalie Wood all spent many happy evenings at Patsy's last restaurant.

When the Godfather of Pizza passed away the family sold the restaurant, and it was declared a Hollywood landmark.

Luckily for California, Patsy and Rose's daughter, Filomena, is following in her parents footsteps. She owns two Italian restaurants, one in the Channel Islands Harbor Food Court. The second, FILOMENA'S VINEYARD CAFE in Oxnard is a classy, sit-down Italian kitchen. Continuing the family tradition, they serve pizza and delicious Italian favorites, many from Patsy's original recipes.

* * * * * * *

Pasta Fagioli

1 1/2 CUPS DRIED CANNELLINI BEANS
  (OR 3 CUPS CANNED)
15 OZ. DRIED SHORT MIXED PASTA
2 CLOVES GARLIC, CHOPPED
1 STALK CELERY, THINLY SLICED
1 SMALL ONION, DICED
4 TBSP. OLIVE OIL
8 OZ. CAN CRUSHED ITALIAN PLUM
  TOMATOES
DRIED BASIL TO TASTE
SALT AND PEPPER TO TASTE

Soak dried beans in water for about 4 hours. Drain and cook in fresh water for 1 hour.

Cook pasta 'al dente'.

Heat olive oil in a large stock pot. Sauté garlic, onion and celery until onion is translucent.

Add tomatoes and basil to taste. Simmer for about 15 minutes.

Stir in cooked beans. If desired, puree some beans to thicken soup.

Add pasta with a little water. Season with salt and pepper to taste.

Serve hot with a sprinkle of grated Parmesan cheese.

* * * * * *

A mixture of different beans make this soup interesting. Try adding kidney and pinto beans for variety.

New York Style Cheese Pizza

THIN CRUST PIZZA DOUGH:
1 TBSP. SUGAR
1 TSP. SALT
1 ENVELOPE (1/4 OZ.) ACTIVE DRY YEAST
1 CUP WARM WATER (110° TO 115°F)
3 1/4 CUPS BLEACHED ALL-PURPOSE
  FLOUR
OLIVE OIL

In a small bowl, dissolve sugar, salt and yeast in warm water. Let sit for 5 minutes.

Add 1 cup of the flour and mix. Add another cup of water and mix until dough comes away from the bowl and forms a soft sticky mass.

Add 1 cup of flour. With your hands, mix flour into dough and remove from bowl and knead.

Add remaining flour and continue kneading until smooth and elastic, about 5 to 10 minutes. Dough will not feel sticky but will be soft. Add more flour if necessary.

Shape dough into a ball. Lightly oil a large bowl. Roll the ball of dough in the bowl to coat it with oil. Seal the bowl with plastic wrap and put in a warm place until dough has doubled in bulk, about 45 to 60 minutes.

Punch the dough down and knead briefly. Let rest 10 to 15 minutes. Lightly coat a 15 to 16 inch pizza screen.

Place dough on a floured surface, press with fingers and dough with hands, keeping dough round until it measures 15 to 16 inches. Place on pizza screen.

TOMATO SAUCE:
   1 CAN (28 OZ.) ITALIAN PLUM TOMATOES
   2 TBSP. TOMATO PASTE
   1 TSP. DRIED BASIL OR OREGANO
   SALT TO TASTE
   PEPPER TO TASTE

Crush tomatoes and combine with tomato paste, basil or oregano, salt and pepper.

Place the desired amount of tomato sauce on top of pizza dough, smoothing out and leaving a 3/4 inch border without sauce.

Top with 3 cups (12 oz.) shredded mozzarella cheese.

Any other toppings may be added, if desired.

Preheat oven to 500° for about 45 minutes.

Place pizza in oven and bake for 10 to 15 minutes until crust is golden brown.

* * * * * * *

In 1939 the Los Angeles Times ran an article announcing that Patsy D'Amore was introducing pizza to Southern California. FILOMENA'S pays tribute to him by offering his favorite pie, Patsy's Special, with pepperoni, sausage and mushrooms.

O'GRADY'S
KANSAS CITY BAR-B-Q

O'GRADY'S KANSAS CITY BAR-B-Q is the "Home of the Famous Tri-Tip Sloppy Joe". This small restaurant occupies a space in the casual food court at Harbor Landing in Channel Islands Harbor.

The menu is classic Bar-B-Q, featuring first quality meats and poultry cooked to perfection. The hardest thing about eating at O'GRADY'S is choosing which mouth-watering meal to dig into. Rotisseried Chicken, Beef and Pork Ribs, Tri-Tip and Hebrew National Dogs are on the menu as well as BBQ Burgers. Baked Potatoes with all the toppings, Chili Fries, homemade Potato Salad and BBQ Beans are just a few of the traditional side dishes that are made fresh daily. The O'Gradys are proud to have won Third Place Overall, the Judges Choice Award, in the 1994 Channel Islands Food and Wine Festival.

Tom O'Grady served as the General Manager before he and his wife, Robin, bought the restaurant from the previous owner in 1993. For many years Tom has created delicious meals for his family and friends, and this new venture has now allowed him to pursue full time his passion for cooking.

The generous portions and Tom and Robin's friendly, outgoing personalities entice local Venturans and many visitors to come back time and time again to O'GRADY'S KANSAS CITY BAR-B-Q.

* * * * * * *

O'Grady's Secret Potato Salad

12 MEDIUM SIZED POTATOES
4 OZ. PIMENTO
3 BUNCHES GREEN ONIONS, CHOPPED
2 CUPS WINE VINEGAR
2 CUPS OLIVE OIL
2 TBSP. SALT
1 TBSP. BLACK PEPPER

Bring a large pot of water to a full boil. Add potatoes that have been peeled and cut in half. Cook for approximately 20 minutes. The potatoes must be cooked through but it is very important that they remain firm to avoid the salad becoming the consistency of mashed potatoes.

While potatoes are cooking, whisk together olive oil, wine vinegar, salt and pepper.

Strain water from the potatoes and cut into 1/2 inch cubes. Stir in pimentos and chopped green onion.

Pour whisked dressing evenly over potatoes and gently stir until completely mixed. It is most important to add the dressing while the salad is still hot in order for the oil and vinegar to properly penetrate the potatoes.

Serves 15 to 20 people.

* * * * * * *

This best ever potato salad is wonderful hot or cold. Unlike many German potato salads, it is not made with bacon so it is a vegetarian dish. It is also a no cholesterol and non-dairy recipe.

THE WHALE'S TAIL

"FOOD AND FUN AT THE WATERS EDGE"

One of Ventura County's finest seafood restaurants, THE WHALE'S TAIL sits on the water in Oxnard's Channel Islands Harbor. The upstairs lounge and shellfish bar is the perfect place to relax and enjoy the spectacular harbor view.

Just inside the front door, the Seafood Market displays fresh, first quality fish, a preview of the menu selection and also available for purchase.

In the downstairs dining room, a wall of glass allows the harbor boats to be seen from every seat in the house. The gleaming, almost life-sized replica of a boat holds the well stocked salad bar. Jaime Ballesteros, the Kitchen Manager for the past 10 years, is the chef responsible for producing creative treats such as Lobster Taquitos. Dinner wouldn't be complete without a trip to their coffee and dessert bar to sample a slice of Barbi's Cheesecake.

The waterfront restaurant is spacious enough for private parties, live entertainment and dancing. The Sunday Brunch is not to be missed.

THE WHALE'S TAIL'S local customers and visitors alike will continue soaking up the fantastic view, delicious food and excellent service for many years.

* * * * * * *

Ceviche

5 LBS. PACIFIC RED SNAPPER (CUT INTO
   1/2 INCH CUBES)
1/2 BUNCH DICED GREEN ONIONS OR
   SCALLIONS
1/2 BUNCH FRESH CILANTRO (CHOPPED)
1 MEDIUM BELL PEPPER (DICED)
2 1/2 CUPS LEMON JUICE
1 1/2 CUPS LIME JUICE
1 TBSP. WHITE PEPPER
1 TBSP. SALT
1 TBSP. GRANULATED GARLIC
1 OZ. TABASCO
2 OZ. SALAD OIL OR CANOLA OIL

In a large bowl, combine lemon and lime juices. Then add white pepper, salt, garlic, Tabasco and salad oil. Mix well.

Add the cubed red snapper, onions, cilantro and bell pepper. Gently mix well.

Refrigerate for 12 hours to blend flavors before serving.

* * * * * * *

Six ounces of Ceviche are served, chilled, on a bed of lettuce with a garnish of fresh lemon slices and a side dish of salsa.

Jaime Ballesteros, Kitchen Manager at THE WHALE'S TAIL restaurant, uses red snapper fresh from local waters.

Angel Hair Pasta
with Lobster

2 OZ. OLIVE OIL
6 OZ. LOBSTER MEAT (WARM WATER OR AUSTRALIAN)
1 TSP. FRESH GARLIC, CHOPPED
4 OZ. TOMATO SAUCE
2 OZ. HEAVY CREAM
1 TSP. FRESH DILL, CHOPPED
4 OZ. FRESH BROCCOLI FLEURETTES
4 OZ. FRESH ANGEL HAIR PASTA (PRE-COOKED 'AL DENTE')

Sauté lobster meat in olive oil until it is about 1/3 done. Add fresh garlic and sauté for one minute more.

Add tomato sauce, heavy cream, chopped fresh dill, broccoli fleurettes and precooked 'al dente' angel hair pasta. Heat through.

Serve promptly. Top with freshly ground black pepper and fresh grated parmesan cheese, if desired.

Makes one generous serving.

* * * * * * *

When available, Jaime Ballesteros of THE WHALE'S TAIL prefers to use fresh lobster caught in local waters.

Fisherman's Wharf is a picturesque New England-style village just right for shopping and dining.

* * * * * * *

CAPTAIN'S GALLEY

The CAPTAIN'S GALLEY offers American favorites and a taste of the Philippines in a comfortable California café tucked inside Oxnard's picturesque Fisherman's Wharf.

The family owned restaurant has been serving up many classic American foods as well as Philippino specialties for more than five years. Tourists and locals may enjoy dining in the fresh air under umbrellas on the patio or indoors in the casual café decorated with classic movie posters and sports photos.

The owners, Mila and Frank Jaramilla, along with their three children, Anthony, Margaret and Frankie create traditional homemade fare including clam chowder, biscuits and gravy, blueberry and honey bran muffins and apple pie. Another of their most popular items is Lumpia, a traditional Philippino egg roll which is also homemade from Mila's own recipe. The "Captain's Favorites" include a variety of sandwiches and burgers.

After an enjoyable meal at the CAPTAIN'S GALLEY, stroll along the Cape Cod-style Wharf, browse through a variety of gift shops and visit The Ventura County Maritime Museum.

* * * * * * *

The 'Perfect' Lumpia

1 LB. GROUND BEEF
1 1/2 CUPS MIXED VEGETABLES
2 TBSP. WATER
1/4 CUP RAISINS
LUMPIA WRAPPERS
EGGS TO SEAL WRAPPERS

Sauté 1 lb. ground beef in a large skillet until it is cooked to medium.

Stir in 1 1/2 cups mixed vegetables and 2 Tbsp. water.

Gently add 1/4 cup raisins.

Place several large tablespoons of the mixture onto each Lumpia wrapper. Brush edges with slightly beaten eggs and roll up starting from one corner (egg roll style).

Submerge completely in medium hot oil and fry until golden brown. Drain well. Serve immediately with hot mustard or sweet and sour sauce.

* * * * * * *

A Lumpia is a traditional Philippino egg roll. The Lumpia wrappers may be found in your grocers freezer. Won ton wrappers may be substituted for Lumpia wrappers.

LOBSTER TRAP

"WHERE THE SUN NEVER SETS"

Thirty years ago, in the heart of the California Gold Coast, a beach resort was just a fantasy. Today, the beautiful Casa Sirena offers gracious hospitality and casual comfort, all in a breathtaking harbor setting. The hotel, at the "Tip of the Peninsula", offers 275 guest rooms, 12 meeting rooms for private social or business gatherings and a large ballroom for banquets.

Visitors never run out of things to do and places to see at the Casa. The sparkling pool, spa, sauna, sun deck, game room, fitness area, putting greens and tennis courts are sure to please. Close by, guests may enjoy shopping or visiting the Maritime Museum at Fisherman's Wharf, touring the Channel Islands, whale watching (seasonal), deep sea fishing and much more.

The LOBSTER TRAP restaurant, at the Casa Sirena Marina Resort, offers a panoramic view of the harbor and meals worthy of a "Captain's Table". Justly famous for the finest in fresh seafood and steaks, it's lavish Sunday Brunch is unforgettable. The restaurant's Oyster Bar serves mouth-watering hot and cold hors d'oeuvres and is an ideal spot to relax. Live entertainment and dancing in the Guadalajara Lounge is perfect for mixing and mingling.

The landmark LOBSTER TRAP restaurant is elegant water side dining and gracious service at it's best!

* * * * * *

96

Award Winning Shrimp Neptune

4 TO 5 STALKS CELERY, CHOPPED
1/2 LARGE ONION, CHOPPED
BUTTER
1 TSP. FRESH GARLIC, CHOPPED
1 TSP. EACH SALT AND WHITE PEPPER
1 TSP. WHOLE THYME
8 OZ. BAY SHRIMP
8 OZ. CRABMEAT
2 CUPS SOURDOUGH BREAD CUBES
1 TSP. PAPRIKA
12 RAW SHRIMP, PEELED, DEVEINED AND
   CUT BUTTERFLY FASHION
12 SLICES RAW BACON

Sauté celery and onion in butter with garlic. Season with salt, pepper and thyme.

When about half cooked, add bay shrimp and crabmeat. Stir in bread cubes and flavor with paprika.

When completely cooked, finely chop or grind stuffing. Allow to cool.

Place a small handful of stuffing into each raw butterflied shrimp and wrap with bacon. For best results, deep fry.

Serve on a bed of rice with cocktail sauce.

* * * * * * *

Chef Bill Reveles of the LOBSTER TRAP is thrilled that this delicious Shrimp Neptune was awarded First Place in the People's Choice at the Channel Islands 1994 Food and Wine Festival.

CAPISTRANO'S

"THE RESTAURANT INSIDE A HOTEL...
NOT A HOTEL RESTAURANT"

CAPISTRANO'S is located inside Oxnard's Mandalay Beach Resort. This elegant restaurant is designed to blend in with the exquisite surroundings of this exceptional beachside hotel.

California cuisine has reached new heights under the guidance of Jean-Claude Guerin, Director of Food and Beverage. He presents a menu filled with gourmet meals prepared from the freshest local ingredients available. Everything is homemade and seasoned to perfection with fresh herbs. Heart smart delicacies are available, such as Bruscetta Capistrano's (fresh tomato, garlic, basil and virgin olive oil on toasted sourdough bread), one of the award winning dishes at the Channel Islands 1994 Food and Wine Festival.

Among the specialties offered at CAPISTRANO'S is the Rum-Glazed Tiger Prawns and the San Francisco-style Dungeness Crab Cakes, both hor d'oeuvres. Entrées, including Shrimp and Scallop Basilic (sautéed with sun-dried tomatoes, shallots, spinach and basil on a bed of linguini) and California Rack of Lamb are served with the chef's selection of fresh seasonal vegetables. Do not miss dessert, the decadent creations are worth it!

Presentation is everything at CAPISTRANO'S. Pleasing the palate and visual satisfaction go hand in hand. From the white linen tablecloths to the meticulously garnished dishes, a treat for the senses is in order. Every meal chosen, whether for lunch or dinner is a culinary delight, to be slowly savored while basking under the care of an attentive server.

* * * * * * *

Rum Glazed Tiger Prawns

5 TSP. CLARIFIED BUTTER
1 1/4 TSP. GARLIC, MINCED
2 1/2 TSP. SHALLOTS, MINCED
30 (16/21) BLACK TIGER SHRIMP
12 OZ. PASSION FRUIT PUREE
20 OZ. PASSION FRUIT VINAIGRETTE
18 RED BELL PEPPER CURLS
18 LYCHEE NUTS
FRESH PARSLEY SPRIGS FOR GARNISH

Place clarified butter in a small hot sauté pan and sauté garlic and shallots. Add shrimp and sauté until they curl. Stir in passion fruit puree.

Remove shrimp and arrange on a serving plate.

Continue simmering vinaigrette, uncovered, until it is reduced by half.

Meanwhile, garnish center of plate with red bell pepper curls and lychee nuts.

Pour vinaigrette over shrimp and garnish lychee nuts with parsley sprigs.

PASSION FRUIT VINAIGRETTE:
1 LB. BROWN SUGAR
1 PINT SEASONED RICE VINEGAR
1 CUP RUM EXTRACT
1 QUART PASSION FRUIT PUREE

Dissolve brown sugar in rice vinegar. Add rum extract and passion fruit puree. Mix until incorporated.

* * * * * * *

Veal Chops
on a Rosemary Stock Reduction

10 OZ. VEAL CHOP
1 TSP. CLARIFIED BUTTER
4 CLOVES GARLIC, CHOPPED FINE
2 BULBS SHALLOTS, CHOPPED COARSE
1 TBSP. FRESH ROSEMARY, CHOPPED
1 CUP BURGUNDY WINE
1 BAY LEAF
1/2 TSP. CRACKED BLACK PEPPER
1/2 GALLON VEAL STOCK
CORNSTARCH SLURRY TO THICKEN
SALT AND WHITE PEPPER TO TASTE

Grill veal chops over medium heat. (About 15 minutes for medium).

Meanwhile, in a large skillet, sauté garlic, shallots and rosemary in butter.

Deglaze (add wine and stir to loosen glaze in the bottom of sauté pan) with burgundy wine and continue cooking.

Add bay leaf and black pepper.

Stir in veal stock and continue cooking, uncovered, until sauce is reduced in volume by 3/4.

If necessary, thicken with cornstarch slurry (a smooth cornstarch and water mixture). Season to taste with salt and white pepper.

Serve veal chop on top of sauce.

* * * * * * *

Baked Apple

5 SMALL APPLES
SUGAR
1 TBSP. BUTTER
1 CUP ONION, DICED SMALL
2 CUPS CELERY, DICED SMALL
1 CUP RAISINS
1 CUP WALNUTS, COARSELY CHOPPED
1 CUP DRIED APRICOTS, COARSELY
   CHOPPED
1/2 TSP. THYME
1/4 TSP. ALLSPICE
1/2 CUP BOURBON WHISKEY
SALT AND WHITE PEPPER TO TASTE

Cut each apple in half from top to bottom. Remove core, scoop out meat and reserve. Coat rims of apple halves with sugar and bake in oven for 10 minutes.

Sauté onions and celery in butter until softened.

Add raisins, walnuts, apricots, thyme, allspice and reserved, chopped apple meat and sauté for one minute more.

Stir in bourbon and burn off alcohol (flambé or raise heat).

Season to taste with salt and white pepper.

Stuff apple halves and serve with veal chops.

* * * * * * *

Strawberry Napoleon

18 WON TON SKINS (3"X3")
1 1/2 PINTS STRAWBERRY FLAVORED
   WHIPPED CREAM
2 CUPS THIN SLICED FRESH STRAWBERRIES
1/4 CUP POWDERED SUGAR
1 CUP SWEETENED WHIPPED CREAM
12 VERY NICE FRESH STRAWBERRY SLICES
6 SPRIGS OF MINT
14 OZ. STRAWBERRY COULIS (SAUCE)

Deep fry won ton skins (keeping them flat) until lightly browned. Place on paper towels to absorb any excess oil and set aside.

On each of 6 serving plates, place 1 won ton skin in the center. From a pastry bag, pipe strawberry cream in a square shape, following the edges of the won ton. Leave the center of the won ton skin hollow.

Fill this hollow space with 1 Tbsp. of the sliced strawberries.

Place another won ton skin gently on top. Repeat the process with the strawberry cream and sliced strawberries and top off with one last won ton skin. Sprinkle with powdered sugar.

Pipe a whipped cream rosette in the center of the top won ton. Garnish with 2 slices of strawberry and a sprig of mint.

Pour strawberry coulis on the plate, around each napoleon.

Serves six.

* * * * * * *

Strawberry Flavored Whipped Cream

2 CUPS HEAVY WHIPPED CREAM
1/2 CUP POWDERED SUGAR
1/4 CUP STRAWBERRY LIQUEUR
1/2 CUP STRAWBERRY FLAVORED MOUSSE
    MIX POWDER OR STRAWBERRY FLAVORED
    SYRUP

In a mixer, whip cream until it starts to thicken, then add all other ingredients. Whip until stiff and cover and refrigerate until ready to use.

* * * * * * *

Strawberry Coulis

1 1/2 CUPS SLICED FRESH STRAWBERRIES
1/2 CUP SUGAR
1 TSP. LEMON JUICE
1/2 TSP. VANILLA
1/2 CUP WATER

Combine all ingredients in a medium saucepan and bring to a boil. Turn down to a simmer and cook for 10 minutes, remove from heat and let cool. Place in blender and puree until smooth. May be strained if desired.

* * * * * * *

Oxnard's Heritage Square is made up of fine original and replicated historical homes.

* * * * * * *

HISTORIC OXNARD

This bustling community, today known as the City of Oxnard, began attracting settlers soon after the founding of the San Buenaventura Mission in the late 1700's. By the end of the next century Port Hueneme was founded by Thomas Bard. This soon became an important shipping outlet for beans, grains, sugar and beets. Achille Levy, a local grain merchant, became a banker. In the late 1800's the Oxnard brothers formed the American Sugar Beet Factory, which would become the second largest in the world. In 1903 this thriving community officially became known as Oxnard and continues to develop and prosper today.

The citizens of Oxnard are working hard to preserve the past. The Maritime Museum traces the story of the channel and coast as far back as 1542, Port Hueneme's Seabee Museum exhibits Navy memorabilia, and the Carnegie Art Museum features local art and historical displays. The unique Gull Wings Children's Museum encourages hands-on experiences such as digging for fossils and discovering how things work.

Oxnard's dedication to never forgetting their roots is most apparent when visiting Heritage Square. This architects dream is made up of fine original and replicated homes which have been moved from other Oxnard locations. The beautiful buildings which date back to the 1800's are surrounded by glorious gardens and house various local businesses. The town plans similar developments for this downtown area. Visitors are welcome to tour the site and may enjoy the free Friday evening open-air concerts.

There is much to be learned about California's colorful past from this multi-cultural community.

* * * * * * *

THE
OYSTER BAY
RESTAURANT

The OYSTER BAY RESTAURANT has been anchored inside the main entrance of the Esplanade Mall since 1970. It was created by Les Valine, father of the present owner, Diane Carr.

Although Diane is now the chief cook and bottle washer, all of the original recipes that her father developed are still served in the restaurant. New England and Manhattan Clam Chowders are homemade daily. Seafood Pan Roast Stews (oyster, shrimp or seafood combinations in a light creamy broth), Seafood Cocktails and salads are served along with the traditional fish frys. Burgers and a full bar are available.

With the best health of her customers in mind, Diane only uses cholesterol-free vegetable oils for frying and has banned MSG and other preservatives. Grilled fish platters are very popular and every effort is made to cater to individual customer's special dietary needs.

No trip to the mall would be complete without a relaxing meal surrounded by warm brick walls adorned with nautical decorations in the OYSTER BAY RESTAURANT.

* * * * * * *

Manhattan Clam Chowder

2 CUPS CARROTS, DICED
2 CUPS CELERY, DICED
2 CUPS ONIONS, DICED
2 GREEN BELL PEPPERS, CHOPPED
1/8 CUP OREGANO
1/8 CUP SALT
1/8 CUP WHITE PEPPER
20 CUPS WATER
23 OZ. CLAM JUICE
2 LBS. CHOPPED CLAMS
4 CUPS PEELED, DICED POTATOES
26 OZ. TOMATO SAUCE
ROUX (SEE RECIPE BELOW)

Combine carrots, celery, onions, bell peppers, oregano, salt, white pepper and water in a large stock pot. Gently boil for about 15 to 20 minutes until carrots are medium soft.

Add the clam juice and chopped clams and continue cooking for 5 minutes.

Add diced potatoes and tomato sauce and cook for about 10 minutes more.

Add the roux slowly, as needed and continue cooking to thicken while stirring occasionally for the last 10 to 15 minutes.

FOR ROUX: Slowly add 3 cups of flour to 1 1/2 cups of salad oil, whipping with a whisk after each small addition of the flour.

Makes about 2 1/2 gallons.

* * * * * * *

YASMEEN'S

INDIAN CUISINE

From the moment one enters YASMEEN'S they are treated to a feast for all the senses. The aroma of fragrant spices escapes from behind a glass wall where meals are prepared for all to see. Mesmerising Indian music plays in the background. Every evening diners are delighted with an intoxicating Indian Dance Show.

The restaurant is tastefully decorated with authentic Indian artifacts. In the foyer, a magnificent, hand-carved elephant table welcomes guests. A collection of brass antiques are displayed in a glass case, and fine artwork depicting the King of India in 1842 hangs on the walls of the dining room. A beautiful, handmade stained glass creation is suspended from the ceiling. One look at the table settings will tell that quality is of utmost importance at YASMEEN'S. The china and crystal are French, the colorful tablecloths are handmade and the chairs are a richly stained cherry.

All meals, including chicken, lamb, beef, seafood, basmati rice and vegetable curries are delicately seasoned with exotic spices. The meats are cooked until tender in the 5000 year old traditional way, using a mesquite clay oven called a tandoor. Naan, a tandoori bread is homemade and freshly baked daily.

Since 1990, this restaurant, named for the owner's young daughter, has provided its loyal customers with fine Indian cuisine. Whether it is for lunch or dinner, visit YASMEEN'S and be treated to superb service, an unforgettable meal and a cool beer or glass of fine wine.

* * * * * * *

Chicken Tikka Masala

4 TBSP. TOMATO PASTE
WATER
1 INCH CUBE FRESH GINGER, PEELED
   AND CRUSHED
1 TSP. GARAM MASALA
3/4 TBSP. SALT
2 FRESH GREEN CHILIES, CHOPPED
1/4 TBSP. VERY SMALL CHOPPED GREEN
   CORIANDER
1 TSP. GROUND, ROASTED CUMIN SEED
1 TBSP. LEMON JUICE
1 CUP WHIPPING CREAM
3 TBSP. UNSALTED BUTTER
20 TO 25 - 2 INCH CUBES OF COOKED
   CHICKEN, BARBECUED IN A TANDOOR
   (CLAY OVEN) OR ROASTED

Combine tomato paste and water together in a mixing bowl. Stir in ginger, garam masala, salt, chopped green chile, coriander, cumin seeds, lemon juice and cream. Mix very well.

Heat butter in a large frying pan, add all the previously mixed ingredients. Bring to a simmer and cook for about 2 minutes over low to medium heat.

Add the chicken pieces, stir once and cook for another 2 minutes.

This dish may be enjoyed with Indian Basmati rice, Pillau or fresh baked bread, Naan. Serves 4 to 6.

* * * * * * *

Garam masala is a mixture of 5 spices including cardamom, cinnamon, cloves and black peppers. It may be found in Indian food shops.

GORILLA GRILL

Anyone with a hearty appetite will find it easily tamed at the GORILLA GRILL restaurant with lots of good food and fast, friendly service! This unique restaurant serves GORILLA-SIZED portions of meat, all barbecued and smoked on an outdoor mesquite-wood barbecue. One factor contributing to the great tasting treats served here are the homemade Oriental-style marinades that the chicken, beef and pork are basted with. In addition to lunch and dinner, they offer a Sunday all-you-can-eat Mexican Brunch and a nightly all-you-can-eat special dinner of BBQ Beef Ribs, Tri-Tip and BBQ Chicken with all the fixings.

GORILLA GRILL patrons can go ape eating on the outdoor patio or in the jungle-like indoor dining room. Large paintings of gorillas hanging on the walls keep customers company while they plow through the huge portions. High ceilings are criss-crossed with wooden beams entwined with vines and spinning ceiling fans. Whimsical stuffed gorillas are tucked here and there. A magnificent 100-year-old wall length side board stands behind the bar where cocktails, beer and wine are served.

The newly remodeled restaurant is family owned and operated by Ted and Virginia Higashi who are also local farmers of some of Ventura's finest strawberries. They extend an invitation to all to take one step into the GORILLA GRILL and go bananas over fabulous food!

* * * * * * *

Pork Cha Shu

CHA SHU MARINADE:
   2 TBSP. SOY SAUCE
   2 TBSP. HOSIN SAUCE
   2 TBSP. BROWN SUGAR
   2 TBSP. COOKING SHERRY
   2 TBSP. HONEY
   1/2 TSP. CHINESE 'FIVE SPICES'
   1/2 TSP. SALT
   1/2 TSP. RED FOOD COLORING,
      OPTIONAL
PORK LOIN STRIPS, 1 INCH THICK

Mix all the marinade ingredients together.

Toss with 1 inch thick pork loin strips to cover completely. Marinate overnight in the refrigerator.

Place pork on a rack over a drip pan and cook in a 325 degree preheated oven for 30 minutes.

Turn and rotate the strips of pork. Baste as necessary and continue cooking for an additional 30 to 40 minutes.

When the cooking is complete the pork should be thinly sliced and served with hot Chinese mustard.

* * * * * * *

Pork Cha Shu is excellent when prepared on a barbecue.

Teriyaki Marinade

1 GALLON SOY SAUCE
5 LBS. SUGAR
1 CUP SAKE OR DRY COOKING SHERRY
12 OZ. KARO SYRUP
3 OZ. THINLY SLICED FRESH GINGER
5 BAY LEAVES

Combine all ingredients in a large saucepan. Heat and stir until the sugar is well blended into the mixture. Do not boil.

Allow sauce to cool. Strain to remove the bay leaves and ginger.

Chicken and ribs should be marinated overnight in the refrigerator. Other meats, such as steaks, require only 1 to 2 hours for marinating.

* * * * * * *

The GORILLA GRILL suggests marinating chicken legs and thighs and barbecuing them for 35 to 40 minutes on a covered grill.

THE OJAI VALLEY

A quaint little town surrounded by rugged mountains is just what the doctor ordered to rejuvenate tired, tense city folk. This artists haven, a short drive inland from the Ventura coast, has enough interesting sights and activities to keep busy all those who want to be entertained, and enough space for loners to escape the demands of everyday life.

It is rumored that almost 130 artists reside in Ojai and many have studios open to the public. On Sunday mornings local artists hold an outdoor exhibit and sale of their works. In the center of town, boutique shopping in the historic Arcade is a favorite pastime of locals and visitors.

Ojai also has it's share of famous resorts. The Oaks, a well known health spa; the Ojai Valley Inn and Country Club, home of the GTE West Classic on the Senior PGA Tour; and Wheeler Hot Springs all draw guests from around the country.

There seems to always be a community festival happening. From the annual Fourth of July Parade to The Ojai, a tennis tournament tradition since 1896, this close knit town welcomes all to attend.

Nature lovers appreciate the many campgrounds, parks and hiking trails available. From sunrise to sunset, boating and fishing are also popular at nearby Lake Casitas.

Ojai Valley residents are proud of their culture and are interested in remembering the past while continuing to look towards the future. Many locals work to maintain this beautiful mountain Shangri-La for all to enjoy.

* * * * * *

L'AUBERGE
RESTAURANT BELGE

The quaint town of Ojai, California's Shangri-La, is the site of well known L'AUBERGE RESTAURANT BELGE. This private home and authentic French restaurant was established by Paul Franssen in 1980. Paul, a former native of Belgium, has a large local following who enjoy dining on the quiet fresh air patio. Lattice work and huge oak trees are a shield against the outside world but do not interfere with the view of the majestic Topa Topa mountains.

Gourmet food lovers and wine connoisseurs travel from afar to dine on fine French-Belgian cuisine and sample superior wines. Each carefully selected item on the menu is homemade and seasoned to perfection by Ted A. Gowrie, the superb Chef de Cuisine for the past 11 years. Patrons are indulged in such exquisite treats as Escalope de Veau Piccata (veal scallops with white wine, lemon and capers), Le Tournedos Auberge (filet sauté garnished with mushrooms and béarnaise sauce), Le Coq au Vin Rouge (breast of chicken with red wine; classic country cuisine) and Scampi á l'ail (shrimp sauté with garlic, tomatoes and herbs).

L'AUBERGE'S gracious host Paul Franssen appreciates the support of his customers and always attempts to make them feel as if they are at his home rather than a restaurant. Fabulous French fare make dining at this grand 1910 country home an unforgettable pleasure.

* * * * * * *

Fresh Mushroom Soup

2 LARGE WHITE ONIONS
A FEW CLOVES OF GARLIC
2 STALKS OF CELERY
OLIVE OIL
1 1/2 LBS. FRESH MUSHROOMS
1 1/2 TSP. DRIED TARRAGON
1 TSP. DRIED THYME
6 CUPS CHICKEN STOCK
2 MEDIUM RUSSET POTATOES
SALT AND WHITE PEPPER TO TASTE

Peel onion and garlic and coarsely chop with celery. Add a small amount of olive oil to a stock pot and cook onions, garlic and celery, covered over low heat until steaming and melted.

Add mushrooms, dried tarragon and thyme and continue to cook, covered, until mushrooms let off water and are simmering.

Add chicken stock, peeled and chopped potatoes, and salt and white pepper to taste. Bring to full boil, then simmer for about half an hour, until potatoes are soft and crumbling.

Let cool slightly and blend until smooth. Return to stove for a second boil and serve.

* * * * * * *

Ted A. Gowrie, Chef de Cuisine, suggests serving this fragrant soup, chilled on a hot summer day with a small amount of cream added.

OJAI VALLEY INN
&
COUNTRY CLUB

Visitors to the famed OJAI VALLEY INN & COUNTRY CLUB will be treated to impeccable service in the elegant Vista Dining Room, a sensational view of the Topa Topa mountains on the Terrace, or a casual meal in the Oak Grill. They may sample delightful cuisine such as Executive Chef Yvan Lampron's Tortilla Soup or Creme Brulee, or Chef de Cuisine, Robert Pugh's Bouillabaisse. Memorable meals are created from the finest, freshest ingredients.

The INN was established in 1923 and is a designated Historic Hotel of America. Its amenities include an 18-hole, par 70 classic golf course; the site of the GTE West Classic Senior PGA Tour Event for the past 18 years. This legendary resort's championship tennis courts have been used by tennis stars Tracy Austin, Jimmy Connors, Billy Jean King and the late Arthur Ashe. Since it's earlist days, the INN has attracted such celebrities as Clark Gable, Lana Turner, and Nancy and Ronald Regan.

The OJAI VALLEY INN has developed Rancho Dos Rios, a 100 acre ranch where hotel guests may now enjoy horseback riding and lessons along the many trails, carriage driving lessons and hayrides. Tiffany, a Chinese potbellied pig and miniature horses are just a few of the friendly animals that delight visitors of all ages at the Children's Farm House.

Whether an overnight guest at the hotel, a day visitor pursuing a passion for golf or a lover of fine cuisine served in an elegant historical setting, there is no doubt that a visit to the OJAI VALLEY INN & COUNTRY CLUB will be an unforgettable experience.

* * * * * * *

Tortilla Soup

3 TBSP. CORN OIL
4 CORN TORTILLAS, COARSELY CHOPPED
6 CLOVES GARLIC, FINELY CHOPPED
1 TBSP. CHOPPED FRESH EPAZOTE (OR
  CILANTRO)
1 CUP FRESH ONION PUREE
2 CUPS FRESH TOMATO PUREE
1 TBSP. CUMIN POWDER
3 TSP. CHILI POWDER
2 BAY LEAVES
4 TBSP. CANNED TOMATO PUREE
2 QUARTS CHICKEN STOCK
SALT TO TASTE
CAYENNE PEPPER TO TASTE
1 COOKED CHICKEN BREAST, CUT INTO
  STRIPS
1 AVOCADO, PEELED, SEEDED AND CUBED
1 CUP SHREDDED CHEDDAR CHEESE
3 CORN TORTILLAS, CUT INTO THIN STRIPS
  AND FRIED CRISP

Heat oil in a large saucepan over medium heat. Sauté the 4 chopped tortillas with garlic and epazote (or cilantro) over medium heat, until tortillas are soft.

Add onion and fresh tomato puree and bring to a boil. Add cumin, chili powder, bay leaves, canned tomato puree and chicken stock. Bring to a boil again, then reduce heat to simmer.

Add salt and cayenne pepper to taste, and cook stirring frequently, for 30 minutes. Skim fat from surface, if necessary.

Strain and pour into warm soup bowls. Garnish each bowl with an equal portion of chicken breast, avocado, shredded cheese and crisp tortilla strips.

* * * * * * *

Bouillabaisse

FOR STOCK:
1/4 CUP OLIVE OIL
1 LARGE ONION, DICED SMALL
1 LEEK, WHITE PART, DICED SMALL
1 FENNEL ROOT BULB, DICED SMALL
4 CLOVES GARLIC, CHOPPED
3 TOMATOES, DICED
2 TBSP. CHOPPED FRESH THYME
2 TBSP. CHOPPED FRESH OREGANO
1 BUNCH FRESH BASIL, CHOPPED
1 CUP WHITE WINE
1/2 GALLON FISH STOCK
2 TBSP. SAFFRON
2 BAY LEAVES
SALT AND PEPPER TO TASTE

SEAFOOD:
2 LBS. FISH FILETS, CUBED
1/2 LB. SEA SCALLOPS
12 LARGE SHRIMP
12 LARGE MUSSELS
12 CLAMS
LOBSTER OR ANY OTHER SEAFOOD

SMALL (BRUNOISE) DICE OF RED, GREEN
AND YELLOW BELL PEPPERS AND ONIONS.

Cook onion, leek and fennel in oil just until soft. Add garlic and cook for 2 minutes more.

Add tomatoes, thyme, oregano, basil, and white wine and cook for 10 minutes on medium heat.

Add fish stock, saffron and bay leaves and bring to a boil. Reduce heat and simmer for 45 minutes. Season to taste with salt and pepper.

In a large pot, sauté fish filets, shrimp, scallops and any other seafood desired. If using a lobster tail, brush with butter and roast in oven 10 minutes.

When seafood is half cooked (about 5 minutes) add brunoise vegetables, bouillabaisse stock, clams and mussels. Cover and cook on medium heat until mussels and clams open.

TO SERVE: Divide seafood and broth between 6 bowls.

BON APPETIT!!

* * * * * * *

This recipe was developed by Robert Pugh, Chef de Cuisine. He has been with the OJAI VALLEY INN since 1993.

Chef Robert most often chooses halibut, swordfish, salmon, ahi and striped bass for the filets in his Bouillabaisse.

Creme Brulee

1 1/4 CUPS HALF AND HALF
3 CUPS WHIPPING CREAM
1 VANILLA BEAN
1 WHOLE EGG
5 EGG YOLKS
1/2 CUP SUGAR
6 TBSP. BROWN SUGAR

In a heavy duty saucepan, scald the half and half, whipping cream and vanilla bean. Cool slightly.

In a separate bowl, mix egg, egg yolks and white sugar together. Add a little of the warm scalded cream to the egg mixture to temper. Mix the tempered mixture back into the cream.

Remove vanilla bean.

Pour mixture into 6 ceramic baking vessels and put on a rimmed sheet pan with a 1/2 inch water bath. Bake at 250 degrees for 45 to 55 minutes. Cool.

Sprinkle 1 Tbsp. of brown sugar evenly over each dish. Caramelize the sugar quickly with high heat (blow torch or flaming broiler). Serves 6.

BON APPETIT!!

* * * * * * *

The OJAI VALLEY INN'S Executive Chef for the past 5 years, Yvan Lampron, uses only the finest, freshest ingredients available to create California Continental Cuisine.

Ojai's original post office, part of Edward D. Libby's beautification program, was donated to the town in 1917.

* * * * * * *

TOTTENHAM COURT LTD.

"TOTTENHAM COURT, a gracious gift emporium and tea shop brings a bit of England to California. It's all lovely", reports Bon Appetit magazine of this enchanting shop located in the heart of The Arcade in Ojai. Various business's have served the community in this spot since before 1910 including a grocery store up until the the 1960's and most recently, just previous to TOTTENHAM COURT, an antique store and flower shop.

This charming Tea Room, with it's reputation for pampering customers, has received the prestigious Fortnum and Mason Award for Excellence in Tea Service, an honor bestowed by the London firm that has been providing foods, wines and provisions to the British Monarchy for almost three centuries. This award, the first to be presented to an eating establishment outside of Great Britain, may be viewed in the shop's front window.

Dining at TOTTENHAM COURT is every bit as delightful as having a leisurely afternoon 'tea' in a real English shop. Freshly made crisp vegetable salads, homemade quiche, flavorful soups and gourmet sandwiches are popular. An old English tradition, The Queen's Own Tea begins with delicate finger sandwiches followed by a Cream Tea with scones, preserves and Devonshire cream, flown in fresh from the English Countryside. A pot of tea or coffee, a 'sweet' and a sherry or mineral water are a perfect ending to England's most civilized ritual.

It is an absolute certainty that dining at TOTTENHAM COURT will be a memorable experience.

* * * * * *

The Queen's Own
Traditional English
Cucumber Sandwiches

1 CUCUMBER (PREFERABLY SEEDLESS)
1 TSP. WHITE WINE VINEGAR
1/2 TSP. SALT
16 SLICES WHITE BREAD
1/4 CUP SWEET BUTTER, SOFTENED

Thinly slice cucumber. Place slices in a colander and sprinkle with vinegar and salt. Let sit for 30 minutes.

Pat cucumber slices dry with a paper towel.

Remove crusts from the bread and lightly butter each slice.

Arrange cucumber slices, overlapping, on half the slices of bread. Cover with remaining bread slices and press together.

Cut each sandwich into thirds. Place on a serving plate and cover with wax paper, then a dampened tea cloth, until ready to serve.

* * * * * * *

Cucumber tea sandwiches are everyone's favorite!

Bread Pudding
with
Chantilly Cream

8 SLICES WHITE BREAD
1 CUP RAISINS
1/2 CUP BUTTER
1 QUART HALF AND HALF
6 EGGS
1 1/2 CUPS SUGAR
1 TSP. VANILLA
ORANGE MARMALADE, OPTIONAL
2 CUPS CHANTILLY CREAM

Cut each bread slice into 4 triangles. Place triangles in 13 x 9 inch baking dish. Scatter raisins over bread. Dot with small pieces of butter.

Bring half and half to a boil. Cool slightly. Beat eggs with sugar and vanilla until light. Gradually stir half and half into egg mixture. Pour evenly over bread. Do not mix.

Bake at 325 degrees for 45 minutes to 1 hour, until golden but not burned. Cool slightly. If desired, spread thin layer orange marmalade over top. Accompany with Chantilly Cream. Makes 12 servings.

* * * * * * *

Chantilly Cream

1 CUP WHIPPING CREAM
1/4 CUP SUGAR
1/4 TSP. VANILLA
1/2 TSP. BRANDY

Combine cold whipping cream, sugar, vanilla and brandy in a bowl and beat until mixture is thick. Cream will not become stiff.

Makes 2 cups. To be served with Bread Pudding.

* * * * * * *

This Bread Pudding recipe was originally made famous by the Bullocks Wilshire Tea Room where it was served for more than half a century until the restaurant closed in 1992.

Ojai's historical Arcade is a favorite shopping area of locals and visitors.

* * * * * * *

OJAI'S COLORFUL PAST

It is believed that 7000 years ago the Oak Grove Indians were the first Ojai Valley residents. The friendly Chumash Indians followed by 1000 A.D. These artistic people lived in peace until the Spanish arrived and introduced devastating diseases that all but wiped out the Indians.

After Mexico gained independence from Spain, the government granted the entire Ojai Valley to Don Fernando Tico for services rendered. In the late 1800's Tico sold the land to entrepreneurs such as R.G. Surdam, who founded the town of Nordoff in 1874. Land at that time went for 45¢ to $1 per acre! The town's name was changed to Ojai (the Chumash translation for 'moon') in 1917.

Also in 1917, the wealthy Edward Drummond Libby built the Ojai Valley Inn and the town center of trade, The Arcade. Although that same year a fire, started in Matalija Canyon swept through the town, the newly built Arcade was spared. Tragedy struck once again a few months later when another fire destroyed half of the arcade shops. It would have been completely destroyed if not for the brick walls of the Ojai Grocery building (now Tottenham Court).

Much of Ojai's fascinating past may be explored in detail in the form of displays and historic photographs in the Ojai Valley Museum.

Many locals and visitors have relived the Valley's lost days while strolling through the now renovated Arcade in the cool evenings. One inescapable pleasure, not widely publicized is the intoxicating scent of orange blossoms from the surrounding orchards. A visit to Ojai is truly a peek into paradise!

* * * * * * *

WHEELER HOT SPRINGS

WHEELER HOT SPRINGS was originally enjoyed exclusively by the native Chumash Indians until the mineral waters were discovered in 1873 by J.W. Wilcox. It has been rejuvenating all who soak in it's mineral-rich, hot spring waters since Wheeler Blumberg built the resort and spa in 1891. Since then it has pampered the elite under the management of a dozen or so different owners, despite being destroyed several times by fires and floods during the past century.

In these modern times, naturally hot and cold mineral waters flow from secluded springs into private tub rooms. Therapeutic massages and skin care services are also available.

The present creekside restaurant and tavern are centered around a huge stone fireplace. Diners may enjoy award-winning European-style cuisine featuring fresh local seafood, first quality meats, fresh herbs and seasonal vegetables. Virtually all food is homemade on the premises including smoked fish and chicken, freshly baked breads and desserts. The hundred-year-old tavern serves premium cocktails and offers an extensive wine list.

A once monthly jazz or blues concert is a popular event that has drawn many fans to this mountain resort located just 6 miles north of Ojai on Highway 33. The rustic decor and friendly, personal service at WHEELER HOT SPRINGS is a perfect remedy for todays hectic lifestyle.

* * * * * * *

Tiramisu

1 BOX LADY FINGERS
BREWED ESPRESSO COFFEE
1 LB. MASCARPONE CHEESE
5 EGGS
3/4 CUP SUGAR
1 SHOT COGNAC
1 SHOT COCONUT RUM
1 PACKAGE GELATIN
POWDERED CHOCOLATE

Separate the egg yolks from the whites.

MIX #1 - Whip the egg whites with 1/2 cup sugar to a firm consistency.

MIX #2 - Whip the egg yolks with 1/4 cup of sugar for about 5 minutes.

MIX #3 - Whip the mascarpone cheese with the cognac and coconut rum for a couple of minutes.

MIX #4 - Mix the gelatin with a splash of warm water.

MIX #5 - Combine MIX #1 with MIX #3.

MIX #6 - Combine MIX #2 with MIX #4 and MIX #5.

First dip the lady fingers in the brewed espresso and then in MIX #6. Place in 3 layers in a square pan. Let set for 6 hours before serving. Serves 8.

* * * * * * *

This delicious dessert is from Chef Gael Leocolley, WHEELER HOT SPRINGS.

RESTAURANT LOCATIONS

VENTURA:

THE PIERPONT INN
550 SAN JON ROAD,
VENTURA, CA. 93001
805-653-6144
BREAK.-LUNCH-DINNER

THE CHART HOUSE
567 SAN JON ROAD,
VENTURA, CA. 93001
805-656-5112
DINNER

NONA'S COURTYARD
    CAFÉ
67 S. CALIFORNIA ST.,
VENTURA, CA. 93001
805-641-2783
BREAK.-LUNCH-DINNER

SHIELDS BREWING CO.,
24 E. SANTA CLARA
    STREET,
VENTURA, CA. 93001
805-643-1807
LUNCH-DINNER
CLOSED MONDAY

CAFÉ VOLTAIRE
34 N. PALM ST.,
VENTURA, CA. 93001
805-641-1743
LUNCH-DINNER

FRANKY'S
456 E. MAIN ST.,
VENTURA, CA. 93001
805-648-6282
BREAKFAST-LUNCH

66 CALIFORNIA
66 S. CALIFORNIA ST.,
VENTURA, CA. 93001
805-648-2266
BREAK.-LUNCH-DINNER

ROSARITO BEACH CAFE
692 E. MAIN ST.,
VENTURA, CA. 93001
805-653-7343
DINNER

CLASSIC CARROT CAFE
1847 E. MAIN ST.,
VENTURA, CA. 93001
805-643-0406
BREAK.-LUNCH-DINNER

TONY'S STEAK &
    SEAFOOD
2009 E. THOMPSON
    BLVD.
VENTURA, CA. 93001
805-643-3322
LUNCH M-F
DINNER NIGHTLY

SEAFARER'S REST.,
450 E. HARBOR BLVD.,
VENTURA, CA. 93001
805-648-7731
BREAK.-LUNCH-DINNER

ERIC ERICSSON'S FISH
    COMPANY
1140 S. SEAWARD AVE.,
VENTURA, CA. 93001
805-643-4783
LUNCH-DINNER
CLOSED MONDAY

THE GALLERY
    RESTAURANT
2055 HARBOR BLVD.,
VENTURA, CA. 93001
805-643-6000
BREAK.-LUNCH-DINNER

FRULLATI'S CAFE DELLA
    RIVIERA
1559 SPINNAKER DR.,
    #109,
VENTURA, CA. 93001
805-658-9153
LUNCH-DINNER M, W-F
B-L-D SAT.-SUN.
CLOSED TUESDAY

ALEXANDER'S
1050 SCHOONER DR.,
VENTURA, CA. 93001
805-658-2000
BREAK.-LUNCH-DINNER

GARFIELDS BAR &
    GRILL
2789 E. MAIN ST.,
VENTURA, CA. 93003
805-648-1917
LUNCH-DINNER

ELEPHANT BAR & REST.
5795 WALKER,
VENTURA, CA. 93003
805-644-6238
LUNCH-DINNER

FLAVOR OF INDIA
1795 S. VICTORIA AVE.,
VENTURA, CA. 93003
805-650-8825
LUNCH-DINNER

OXNARD:

BARBI'S BAKERY
2810 S. HARBOR BLVD.,
OXNARD, CA. 93035
805-985-0527
BREAKFAST-LUNCH

CHUY'S & KONA RANCH
    HOUSE
2800 S. HARBOR BLVD.,
OXNARD, CA. 93035
805-985-0996,985-5723
CHUY'S:L-D, DAILY
KONA: L-D, CLOSED
    MONDAY

FILOMENA'S PIZZA
2810 S. HARBOR BLVD.,
OXNARD, CA. 93035
805-984-6388
LUNCH-DINNER

FILOMENA'S VINEYARD
    CAFE
2550 VINEYARD AVE.,
OXNARD, CA. 93030
805-983-7395
LUNCH-DINNER

O'GRADY'S KANSAS CITY
    BAR-B-Q
2810 S. HARBOR BLVD.,
OXNARD, CA. 93035
805-984-2088
LUNCH-DINNER

THE WHALE'S TAIL
3950 BLUE FIN CIRCLE,
OXNARD, CA. 93035
805-985-2511
LUNCH-DINNER

OJAI:

CAPTAIN'S GALLEY
3900 W. CHANNEL
    ISLANDS BLVD.,
OXNARD, CA. 93035
805-985-7754
BREAK.-LUNCH-DINNER

LOBSTER TRAP
3605 PENINSULA RD.,
OXNARD, CA. 93035
805-985-6311
LUNCH-DINNER

CAPISTRANO'S
2101 MANDALAY BEACH
    ROAD,
OXNARD, CA. 93035
805-984-2500
LUNCH-DINNER

THE OYSTER BAY REST.,
213 ESPLANADE DR.,
OXNARD, CA. 93030
805-485-2657
LUNCH-DINNER

YASMEEN'S INDIAN
    CUISINE
2311 OXNARD BLVD.,
OXNARD, CA. 93030
805-485-3804
LUNCH-DINNER

GORILLA GRILL
2639 WAGON WHEEL
    ROAD.,
OXNARD, CA. 93030
805-983-3474
LUNCH-DINNER

L'AUBERGE RESTAURANT
    BELGE
314 EL PASEO,
OJAI, CA. 93023
805-646-2288
DINNER WED.-MON.
LUNCH SAT.-SUN.

OJAI VALLEY INN &
    COUNTRY CLUB
COUNTRY CLUB ROAD,
OJAI, CA. 93023
805-646-5511
BREAK.-LUNCH-DINNER

TOTTENHAM COURT
    LTD.,
242 E. OJAI AVE,
OJAI, CA. 93023
805-646-2339
LUNCH

WHEELER HOT SPRINGS
16825 MARICOPA HWY.,
OJAI, CA. 93023
805-646-8131
DINNER THURS.-SUN.
BRUNCH SAT.-SUN.

*MANY RESTAURANTS
SERVE A SUNDAY
BRUNCH. CALL TO
INQUIRE.

FOR FURTHER INFORMATION

VENTURA VISITORS & CONVENTION BUREAU
89 S. CALIFORNIA ST.,
VENTURA, CA. 93001
805-648-2075

CHAMBER OF COMMERCE GREATER VENTURA
785 S. SEAWARD AVE.,
VENTURA, CA. 93001
805-648-2875

VISITOR INFORMATION-TOURISM OXNARD
711 SOUTH A STREET,
OXNARD, CA. 93030
805-385-7545

CHAMBER OF COMMERCE OXNARD
400 E. ESPLANADE DR.,
OXNARD, CA. 93030
805-485-5255

CHAMBER OF COMMERCE OJAI VALLEY
338 E. OJAI AVE.,
OJAI, CA. 93023
805-646-8126

ORDER A COOKBOOK FOR A FRIEND!

Please send me _____ COOKIN' IN VENTURA cookbook(s) at $9.95 plus $2. shipping and handling each. Include sales tax where applicable. CA. residents pay 7 1/4%. Check or money order only, please.

MAIL TO: GOLD COAST PRESS,
          4360 E. MAIN ST., SUITE 129,
          VENTURA, CA. 93003

NAME:

ADDRESS:

CITY: STATE: ZIP:

FOR MORE INFORMATION 805-642-6346. 8AM-5PM.

ORDER A COOKBOOK FOR A FRIEND!

Please send me _____ COOKIN' IN VENTURA cookbook(s) at $9.95 plus $2.00 shipping and handling each. Include sales tax where applicable. CA. residents pay 7 1/4% Check or money order only, please.

MAIL TO: GOLD COAST PRESS,
          4360 E. MAIN ST., SUITE 129,
          VENTURA, CA. 93003

NAME:

ADDRESS:

CITY: STATE: ZIP:

FOR MORE INFORMATION 805-642-6346. 8AM-5PM.